A future-oriented season
The first season of Brendan Rodgers as Liverpool FC manager. A personal account

Pablo Gutiérrez

Ediciones La Catedral y La Colina
Madrid

Copyright © 2013 Pablo Gutiérrez

All rights reserved. No part of this book may be reproduced in any manner whatsoever without written permission except in the case of brief quotations embodied in critical articles and reviews. For information, contact the author at pgflfc@hotmail.com

ISBN: 978-1490533971

Contents

PROLOGUE 7
INTRODUCTION.- A future-oriented season 9
1.- Back in football business, hopes and fears..............15
2.- Looking at the future 20
3.- Merits, achievements, frustrations, justice 24
4.- Good week and football thoughts exposed 28
5.- Luck, history, balance 33
6.- Depth and width 38
7.- Up and coming 43
8.- Ambition, realism..48
9.- A match with a bit of everything.............................52
10.- Where football is 57
11.- The Audacity of Hope 62
12.- Versatility, confusion 67
13.- Calmed victory 71
14.- Same eleven, worse result 75
15.- Endless (yet interesting) debates 80
16.- More growing opportunities 85
17.- Penalties shoot-outs and lessons to learn 90
18.- Dickensian match 95
19.- Similar beginnings, different endings 99
20.- Getting ready for prime time 103
21.- New Year balances and wishes 107
22.- Winning by the book 111
23.- All's well that ends well? 115
24.- Still not there 120
25.- Wish you were here...124
26.- Hitting the woodwork..128
27.- "Yes, but no" 132
28.- Costly mistakes 136
29.- Football is sometimes…football 140

30.- "Know thyself": classic piece of advice and modern day football 145
31.- Useless goals 150
32.- Playing anywhere 155
33.- Big players making themselves count 160
34.- Winning wings 165
35.- Ongoing lessons 170
36.- Self-awareness 175
37.- Resigning, retiring 180
38.- Slow and steady progress 185
39.- Aphorisms and football wisdom 189
40.- Player selection and game plan 194
41.- Taking the difficult path 199
42.- The hero that was on time 204
44.- Woodwork, again 209
CONCLUSION.- Player by player season assessment .. 214

PROLOGUE

It is often said that one of the traits of Liverpool FC fans is our desire to keep in touch with each other, to debate, to discuss, to share ideas about the team, the players, the city, our club, football in general, other clubs, and so on.

One can check this by checking the vitality of forums or blogs all around the internet, in which all kinds of issues relating, more or less closely, LFC, are endlessly discussed. In this book I present the posts I have been uploading about 12/13 LFC season.

Most of these posts have been posted during the season to the club page social network, "The kop"; others have been posted elsewhere. I have fully enjoyed the experience of writing the posts, and sharing my views with fellow Liverpool FC fans, and with the comments and replies I have had.

In the process of preparing the articles to be published in this book I have added some contextual information (date of the post, and results of matches involved). I have also written some added contributions. But this book is mostly about my views as 12/13 season unfolded.

I have made some minor editing and corrected some mistakes. Even so, it surely remains obvious that English is not my first language, and I apologize in advance for that. I hope that language mistakes do not obscure my views and what I have tried to express, and are not excessively annoying for English speakers.

Other than those minor corrections, the articles remain as I wrote them in the date given. Subsequent developments might have both proved me wrong in some issues and right in other ones, but I have not taken advantage of the hindsight to correct my views. In that sense, this set of articles can be viewed as a diary in its own right, even if not totally steady, as there are some voids in the articles.

Even so, majority of the season and main issues regarding LFC are, some way or another, covered. There are also some references to youngsters and the Academy, and even to some aspects of football in general. But the main character of the book is, indisputably, the first squad of Liverpool FC and its 12/13 season.

A season that from every corner of the club has been considered future-oriented. As such, only time will tell in what regard it should be considered by fans. In the meantime, these articles sum up what the season has been like from the standpoint of a particular fan. Now, it is for the readers to judge whether or not that standpoint is of any interest. But it is surely one expression of that desire that LFC fans share to have their views known, and to debate about their beloved club.

INTRODUCTION.- A future-oriented season

At the end of 2011/2012 season, LFC directors decide to part company with Kenny Dalglish and to sign as the new manager a young, energetic, and prestigious Northern Ireland man, Brendan Rodgers. Rodgers had done a terrific work over precedent seasons with Swansea, had had a spell as coach in Chelsea, and overall had had quite a long managerial career for someone his age.

LFC directors deemed unacceptable a 52-point, eighth position, finish in the Premier League. Outstanding domestic cup performances and successes, including winning the league cup (meaning qualification for European competition) and being finalists of the FA cup, were not enough for them. But it was probably more of a general situation issue than mere results.

Directors and owners wanted seemingly to instil new direction, new leadership, into the team. Dalglish had done a great job in rescuing the team from a bad situation in January 2011, and achieved not only cup success, but also a not title-winning, but somewhat remarkable, tally of 67 points in his 38 first Premier League games, in the second half of 2010/11 season and the first half of 2011/2012 season. But the 18 points achieved in his last 18 league games were far from what LFC should aim for and signalled a low point in team form.

So LFC owners gave the realms to Brendan Rodgers, with mixed outcomes. In cup competition, 2012/13 season has been weak; a home defeat at Anfield against Fulham in the league cup; an away defeat against Oldham, both in second round appearances. And an elimination in Europa League against Zenit in the first knock-out round. All cup competitions have been disappointing throughout the season.

League wise, 61 points mean a clear improvement on previous season while still at least 10 points short of the very minimum LFC should collect every season. 7th place is a shy improvement on previous season, but not even close to enough for LFC.

However, there have been another encouraging signs. The level shown on the pitch by the team has been more consistent and of more quality than in the second half of 2011/12 season. There is a general consensus on the current squad being better, in quality and depth, and with a clearer path to improvement now than prior to the arrival of Rodgers.

And, for better or worse, that has been the message during all season from LFC headquarters. Time and again, Rodgers has been speaking about the building process, the work in progress, the road behind and ahead, the partial achievements, the planned way forward, and the like. Since the beginning, we LFC fans were told that the season was only a first step, and that there were better things to come, given the appropriate time for squad and team to develop.

Of course, there is always the question about if something like a "transitional season" could, or should, even "exist" for a club like LFC; but, as of now, it is more a question of "how many" transitional seasons remain ahead for the club, since LFC is in effect on a transitional period since the dismissal of Benitez, now three years ago.

As such, the season and merits of Rodgers should possibly be assessed on the basis of the progress made to date. From that standpoint, Rodgers has at least achieved the minimum in terms of objective data, with the 7th place and the 61 points, even if cup competitions have been elusive.

On top of that, progress in terms of squad building seems a reality. Especially after January, in which the additions of Coutinho and Sturridge look, as of now, master strokes in the transfer markets. Of course there has to be some prevention, as they both need to prove their worth on a long term basis. But, for the time being, they have enormously added to the team and squad.

Those January addition's effects can be seen on the results; after 25 points in first 19 league games (a "hodgsonian" tally), 36 points in the second half of the season, for a total of 61, might point to a better future, to a real work not only in progress but in fact progressing. Still, it is worth it remembering that in the much criticised last season under Benitez the team achieved 63 points, deemed unacceptable at the time.

Again, it is important not to lose track on the big picture. LFC have clearly improved on the second half of the season. Not only Coutinho and Sturridge have played their part; Reina has played significantly better in the second half of the season; Johnson and Enrique have been more comfortable, and Agger has had his best season injury wise. Leiva has been settling after his long injury, and Gerrard has had a great season, with Henderson and Downing getting close to the players Dalglish thought he had signed, and Suarez at his usual astonishing level, even improving his goal scoring ability, helping the team to dramatically improve the amount of league goals scored, from 47 to 71.

Perhaps more important, the team as a whole seems to be adapting to Rodgers, and vice versa, gaining in consistency and reliability. Even more, achieving the ability to compete in all sorts of circumstances, including the ban on Suarez or the injuries to Agger and Gerrard in last games of the season. Granted, much more progress is needed, but it seems to be little doubt that Rodgers has deserved another season to keep on with his building work.

Another season that might be more difficult; he will need to be inch-perfect in his transfer decisions on the summer, both in the arrivals and the outings, to strengthen the squad in the appropriate ways. In 2013/2014 season the team needs to be, at the very, very least, challenging for a top four spot. On one hand, LFC should not be more years left out of the Champions League; on the other hand, there should be no reasons for LFC to keep steadily ending below Everton, Tottenham, or Arsenal season after season.

Of course, in the brief look at the players above, there is one outstanding absence. He is the big character in this future-oriented season. Jamie Carragher has decided to call time on his conspicuous LFC career. And what a way of saying goodbye. He has been an absolute rock in the defence since his comeback to the team in January.

He has to show not only his long years of outstanding service, or his list of titles won; he has been a key figure in the team for the entire second half of the season. It is not exactly that he retires on his peak (in fact, that is neither possible nor desirable), but he retires being a key piece on the team, an automatic starter of the matches, a real factor in the improvement of the team in his last months as LFC player.

This season, oriented from the beginning to the future, has had as one of his main characters a long time servant to the club. Once Carragher has rendered his last, and valuable, service, the team should make this season look good in retrospective by offering a great next season. That is the enormity of the challenge that Rodgers faces: next season will decide not only if next season is good in itself; it will also determine if this 2012/2013 has been good enough for LFC, if his appointment makes sense in the long term.

1.- Back in football business, hopes and fears

Date: 13/09/12
Previous matches: Gomel 0-1 LFC (Uefa Europa League); LFC 3-0 Gomel (Uefa Europa League); West Brom 3-0 LFC (Premier League); Hearts 0-1 LFC (Uefa Europa League); LFC 2-2 Man City (Premier League); LFC 1-1 Hearts (Uefa Europa League); LFC 0-2 Arsenal (Premier League)

Football holidays are well passed now, and new season is under way. As it has become a norm in recent years, we are handed an early pause that allows for some thinking and reflection on where we are with still nearly all season ahead. After some emotional days for LFC fans and the releasing of Hillsborough report, I wanted to have my say on football matters, how 12/13 season looks as of now, what can be made of last summer transfer window, and the initial steps of Brendan Rodgers as LFC manager.

Obviously, they are three closely interrelated issues, so in the end it is difficult to speak of the separately of them; but, for the sake of some order, I will try to focus on one issue at a time. To start with, the perspectives on current season. Seven official matches have already been played, three of them in the Premier League and four in the Europa League. I would say that at first sight there are more reasons for concern that for optimism: in the Europa

League the main goal, getting through to group stages, has been achieved. However, it has been achieved with one good game (at home against Gomel) and three relatively flat games. Notwithstanding that, the truth is that the team has got through and the timing of the matches was tricky, so to certain extent it was satisfactory, and some optimism can compensate the concern.

Similarly in the Premier League, where it is clear that the final scores have not been good. But the team have probably deserved a little bit better. Against West Bromwich, the first half was more or less OK for a first match of the season; after that, the team collapsed and ended almost embarrassingly, not because of the attitude or the commitment, but for the lack of competitiveness in the players and the team as a whole, the poor handling of the match circumstances. Against Man City, LFC were head and shoulders above their rivals, and should have run out comfortably winners, had it not been for blatant defensive mistakes. Not bad luck, but bad mistakes, which is not exactly the same. Against Arsenal, LFC were simply second best in the day. Two similar teams with similar game plans, but, in that match, Arsenal were better and deservedly won the match. There is no hiding, though, that there was not that much separating the two teams, and that the gap between them does not seem to be insurmountable.

Overall, hence, few games, but still enough to start knowing the team. LFC have shown certain glimpses of new ways of playing, certain spells of good performances, and some encouraging signs. Along with that, the team has also shown worrying weaknesses in defence, and inconsistency during the matches. Furthermore, both owner and manager have more or less publicly accepted certain shortage in number of players, coming from last season. Which leads me to the transfer market. During summer, LFC have lost Maxi, Kuyt, Adam, Spearing, and Carroll (Aquilani was loaned out last season, so he is not a "loss" when comparing to last season; he is certainly a loss regarding his footballing qualities, but that is another question); they have been replaced by Sahin, Allen, Borini, Cole, Sterling, Assaidi (as of now, I doubt if Pacheco will be used enough to be counted here). So, in terms of squad structure, of positions of the players, things are similar.

Not so, I hope, in terms of quality. I think that Sahin/Allen are a clear improvement on Spearing/Adam; Cole/Sterling should be capable of also improve over Maxi/Kuyt; Borini is clearly a different type of striker from Carroll, and is the sign of a different approach to the game by the manager. But apparently Rodgers wanted to replace Carroll with another striker, and couldn't, so it was possibly never the intention to replace Carroll with Borini. I honestly don't have as of now enough information about the potential role and importance of Assaidi. So, generally speaking, the squad has been improved over last season. Whether that improvement is an adequate reflection of the money spent, or if the money could have been spent in a more cost effective way is much more difficult to say.

However, I think that certain weaknesses in the squad have not been dealt with. My main concern is not really the attacking side of the game. In my view, Allen, Sahin, Gerrard, Shelvey, Henderson, Downing, Cole, Sterling, Borini, Suarez are more than capable of creating problems to any defence. Truly at least one addition is needed (maybe Carroll himself, given the time to develop his game and confidence elsewhere), and I am not as blind as to think they are the best striking force in the Premier League, but they are certainly one the rivals should be afraid of. I think that the real weakness of the squad is in the defensive side, specifically in the centre of the defence. I have already expressed this point of view, and I think it is telling that seven goals have been conceded in three Premier League games, of which at least four were preceded by some type of serious defensive mistake, either individual or collective.

It is urgent, and getting even more urgent by the day, to sign at least one top class central defender. Agger is one of them, no doubt; but he cannot play every game at the top of his form, and needs a partner near his level. Skrtel can help, but he is not a top quality centre back, and cannot play as left central defender (as seen against Man City). Carragher can also be of help, but he is not getting better now. Maybe the hope is that Coates will dramatically improve his level, which would be great news for LFC. Otherwise, signing action is needed here, and it is a precondition for LFC to really improve its league form.

Being things as they are, I am afraid that 4th spot will be extremely difficult to achieve, and probably a more realistic goal for the end of the season is 5th or 6th. And a good run in the cups, of course. In any given day, this team can face and beat any other, as seen against Man City, and cup form could benefit from it; equally, if things go wrong, this team can lose against almost any other team (as seen against West Brom). But, being important, results are not everything. And there is well founded hope, that I also have, that the team can improve the quality of the play, can keep improving the path already started last season of keeping the ball, dictating the game, owning the matches. A hope of approaching the passing game of the great LFC teams.

I like how the Rodgers' words sound. I like his approach to the game, and I like what he has set as his goal of developing a team that is in charge of the matches through the ball and through being ambitious. It will no doubt take time, but if during the season that can be in fact seen, and not only talked about, it is likely that we LFC fans can have good moments. If come May clear improvement can be seen on that front, and league form is better than last season, if the team shows a clear path forward, the season could end up having been a good one, despite this somewhat disappointing start.

2.- Looking at the future

Date: 20/09/12
Previous matches: Chelsea U21 1-4 LFC U21 (U21 League)

While it is impossible to predict the future, football fans are always trying to do it, through all kinds of football strategies: historic precedents, luck (or bad luck) omens, indescribable feelings assuring something great or terrible is going to happen,...I like to think that looking at the matches of youth teams of the club is a more "scientific" way of predicting.

I am very much afraid that it is not; that much as one may pay attention to youth teams, it is not a clear indication of the future of the first team. But, anyway, I like to do it. And if some of my own "predictions" happens to become true (believe it or not, it has happened), I feel very proud. Needless to say, if a prediction fails to fulfil, it will never be my fault. Certain circumstances would have prevented my prediction from becoming a reality.

So last Friday I decided to see the U21 Chelsea-LFC match ready to draw some conclusions on players, systems, and the near future of LFC squad. And I have to say it was a very good display by the team, against a strong opposition.

To begin with, Gulacsi seems to have learned one of the outstanding traits of Reina: his distribution of the ball; when the chance aroused, he put the football in play quickly, and almost always accurately, both in the choice and the precision of the pass. It allowed the team to start the play with advantage in many an occasion.

Centre-backs Sama and Wisdom were not very much tested, which is a credit to the team, and looked comfortable when called into action, with the exception of Chelsea goal. But not many conclusions could be obtained from that match in that front.

Full backs Smith and Robinson looked to a certain extent shy in the attacking, and experienced some troubles in defending, especially Smith. But to their credit his help was not much needed in attack, and they were able to maintain their composure under the circumstances, and ended up getting the better of their opponents. Not to forget that Smith was confronted with Marko Marin, one of the European hottest prospect, and a full international with Germany.

In the centre of midfield Coady and Roddan managed the match and were better than their counterparts. Coady, though having played fine, was not at his very best, but Roddan more than made amends for it, and played one of his best matches in an LFC shirt. Hopefully he can keep improving and making his impression on matches.

On the flanks, Morgan and Pacheco both played very well, and added to the team performance. Morgan was a constant threat to opposite goal, even if he lacked a bit of accuracy, and was a nightmare to Chelsea defenders with his mobility and pressing, while offering chances to their team mates for passes. Pacheco was probably the best player, unstoppable for the Chelsea defenders, running time and again through the left flank and providing with more than decent crosses. Very good to see him near to his best.

Behind the strikers, Adorjan gave a very good account of himself, constantly in contact with the football, moving, passing, keeping a high tempo and with a very good eye for passes.

Finally, Yesil played his first match for LFC, and looked a very good prospect, a lively forward with his eyes firmly on opposite goal, great mobility, and a more than fine technique. He needs to improve his knowledge of the game and team mates, but could be very helpful for the U21 and even for the first team in relatively short term.

When called into action, Ngoo did also well, inflicting damage on the Chelsea defence with his prowess and speed.

Overall, great display by the team, especially in a very good second half. They only lacked a little bit of match control, of keeping hold of the football when the chance to get forward was not clear, and at certain moments more help in defence to the full backs. And, well, the result is also important in competitive football, and a 4-1 win away against Chelsea, current Youth Cup champions, is worth mentioning.

Very different issue is if, and when, any of these players will be helpful additions to the first team. On that front, I would say that in the short term Pacheco, Morgan and

Yesil seem to be the better options, other than Robinson that has already appeared in the first team. Anyway, Rodgers has proved that he is ready to hand chances to the youngsters if he feels they are prepared, so who knows?

Good match in this starting season. Let's see if the players and staff can build on it and keep developing their footballing skills and becoming better players as individuals and also better team as a whole.

Meanwhile we fans will as likely as not keep making predictions about what the future holds for LFC, and forgetting those predictions when we have the occasion of making new ones. But, at the same time, we all are aware that in very rare occasions one single match is enough to make informed predictions. So I will keep an eye on the U21s during the season. At the very least, I am certain that they will provide good moments of football, and that is, after all, the real reason why we see football.

3.- Merits, achievements, frustrations, justice

Date: 24/09/12
Previous matches: Sunderland 1-1 LFC (Premier League); Young Boys 3-5 LFC (Uefa Europa League); LFC 1-2 ManU (Premier League)

It is becoming (indeed, it has become) conventional wisdom that LFC is playing much better football than the league table reflects. The achievements (a mere 2 points after 5 league games) don't match the merits of the team in terms of level of play, goal chances for and against, handling of the football,…As I see it, that much is true. However, dwelling on bad luck is not productive, and some lessons can be drawn from these first matches. In the end, there is room for improvement, and improving must be the target.

As said above, I very much agree with LFC having been undone by the league results so far. Instead of 2 points, the minimum LFC have deserved is 5 points (a win against Man City, and draws against Sunderland and ManU), and 9 points would have not been totally undeserved (3 wins in those matches). Against West Brom and Arsenal the defeats reflected what happened on the pitch. Even if the first half against West Brom was not too bad; but, on the whole game, the defeat was fair.

I was left particularly frustrated after ManU game. I saw no reason whatsoever to explain the victory of the rivals. I could have coped with a draw, frustrating as it would have been; but a defeat was way too much, given that LFC completely outplayed the opposition before the red card to Shelvey, and even after it the match was about even, if not leaning LFC. Overall, LFC were clearly the best team, and somehow left the pitch defeated. The match was possibly the best example (not the only one) of how much does it take for LFC to score, and how little does it take for them to concede.

Admittedly, LFC were head and shoulders above ManU during the first half; however, there were not that many clear cut chances to score. That is something that needs to be improved. The ability to transform the bossing of the game in clear chances to score, and convert those chances. The only game in which the team excelled at that front was the 5-3 win against Young Boys; for a change, LFC scored more than they really deserved on that match. Even so, for long spells the match was similar to the rest of matches of the season, until in the final minutes Shelvey took the pitch by storm, looking like a man playing literally against "young boys".

The first half against West Brom, or Sunderland and Man City matches, the team was better, was dominant, played a fairly good football. Not brilliant, but good. However, in those occasions, as in the match against ManU, the players failed to really create as many goal chances as the games demanded. Two different reasons might be responsible for that. On one hand, the team is still adjusting to a new manager, a new way of playing, new concepts,…and also new players; hopefully this front can be worked on in the following weeks, and improvement can be seen sooner than later. On the other hand, a striker is missed, at least in certain moments of games, when more presence in opposition box is needed. It is no secret that Rodgers tried to sign a replacement for Carroll and it was not possible. This front is much more difficult to address in the short term; other than Morgan or Yesil stepping in and taking a giant step forward, it won't be until January or even next summer than action can be taken here. Even so, I trust the current squad to provide enough goals to stand the team in good stead, if some improvement could be seen in defence.

Hence, I find it much more worrying the problems in defence. It seems painstakingly easy for rivals to score against LFC, and it has been so in every match (other than the first rounds of Europa League). There are two sides of it: the fact that mistakes are made by LFC defenders in every match, and the fact that almost every mistake seems to be penalised by a goal. In the later, bad luck can have a part; in the former, not. So that is what needs to be solved and fixed. Against ManU, one man down, few minutes after Gerrard's goal, Rafael got in LFC box and Agger failed to close his shot angle. It was a soft mistake, one that would have gone unnoticed almost every time, but somehow Rafael managed to draw a goal from that extremely difficult shot. To a great extent, bad luck. But not only bad luck.

LFC defenders are making more mistakes than they are expected to (in all fairness, they are expected to make no mistakes at all, but, well, I mean their fair share of mistakes). And blaming it only on bad luck is not going to help. I guess that some corrections might be possible through training and keeping focused. But in all likelihood it will take new players to get into the team, particularly in the centre of defence. And, after last news about Kelly (arguably the best player against ManU, although I have not seen him especially praised) and Agger (the best defender in the squad) going to be sidelined for long spells, it will take great management by Rodgers to really improve the defence of the team. And that will be necessary to improve the results.

All in all, I hope the team will be able to keep improving its midfield play, as the players grow more and more comfortable with Rodgers style of play. In doing so, LFC will keep conveying the impression to deserve victories, as they are likely to be dominant in most matches. But action needs to be taken in both boxes. In defence, reducing the mistakes and being more assured; in attack, turning the good play in goal chances. That is as far as the team can go; if afterwards bad luck keeps appearing, then so be it. Sooner or later, Lady Luck will begin going LFC way. But the team needs to work on what they can improve, and get ready for the moment in which the luck turns and frustrations end.

So this is it for merits, achievements, frustrations. The "justice" in the title of the post is obviously a tribute to the Hillsborough 96 and their families in these so significant days. Congratulations for the truth being at last public knowledge. YNWA.

4.- Good week and football thoughts exposed

Date: 29/09/12
Previous matches: West Brom 1-2 LFC (League Cup)

A very good win by LFC against West Brom en route to a come-back to Wembley. Very good win, that is, that left very good news. And also very interesting points. And, to close the circle, some not-so-good news. Anyway, overall, a good match, with good performances, and an undisputable step forward in the season.

When a manager decides to field a second-string team (and that was the case against West Brom, with eleven new players compared to the ManU game), it allows the observer to go deeper in his football thoughts. It becomes clear that the structural things that remain the same once all the players have been changed should be what the manager asks his players to do. Of course, there are other occasions in which one could get to know the football thoughts of the manager, but this match provided that valuable insight in his ideas.

Not that we learnt anything particularly new, or unexpected: keep hold of the football, control the game, extensive use of the wings, mobile centre-forward, good transitions of the ball between defence and midfield, and between midfield and attack; in defence, press on the ball, keep the team compact, coverings between players, and alternate between pressing up the pitch and waiting in own half.

The defensive side of the game worked well, generally speaking. It took some minutes for the players to adjust, which is completely understandable, and it was punished by the West Brom goal, and a good chance by Lukaku shortly afterwards. But, other than that and the late woodwork, the defenders handed well the challenges. Wisdom and Robinson were solid, and Coates and Carragher dominated their rivals. Tactically, it was interesting that Carragher played on the left, which may be a hint that Rodgers is thinking in him to replace Agger. He looked focused and bossing the field. Coates played well; still, I keep the impression that he doesn't really impose his physical strength when in defence, looking sort of shy at times. Oddly enough, he is not hesitant at all to impose his presence in the opposition box, where he is a constant threat.

When attacking, the team showed the same kind of virtues and problems than the "first team". The main problem is the lack of presence on opposition box. A direct consequence of the intentions of the team. The option for filling the midfield with players to control the football and the rhythm of the match, while at the same time keeping players wide open in the wings has the consequence of having few players getting into the box. That of course can be contra rested in some ways, and Rodgers is no doubt working on it on the training pitch. But, as of now, it is a constant trait of the team.

A trait that to an extent (I would say that to a great extent) accounts for the difficulties the team is experiencing to transform the control of the games into a real clear cut goal chances. One problem is the general lack of accuracy in the crosses; that is not, obviously, a tactical choice. But it is something that LFC players should work on in training. It happens often that a good combination leads to a good crossing position that is squandered by a bad cross. But there are also tactical adjustments to try to make up for the lack of presence in the attacking box.

It is possible to have a powerful striker who can almost by himself cause problems to defenders; that is, a Crouch, a Carroll, a Dzeko,…The type of striker that, even if with no other team-mates near him, can either shot or keep the ball while help arrives. Rodgers has obviously discarded this option for the moment. There is other option, the one that uses Barcelona, or Arsenal, which is trying to go through the centre of the field, and using the wings only as a resource and a way to open defences; more importantly, using the wings mainly with full-backs, and not wingers.

This approach seems to be the main option for Rodgers. When playing the "first unit", Kelly and Johnson have had a continuous presence on opposition half; and, even if Sterling is playing as a winger, he is increasingly getting towards the box. With the injury to Kelly, it is likely that Johnson will turn to the right with Enrique on the left, hence keeping the use of full-backs in attack. That was something barely seen against West Brom, with Wisdom and Robinson seldom getting on the attack.

There is a third possibility, probably the most obvious though also the most dangerous. If the players are occupying positions in midfield and the wings, and more players are needed in the box, let the holding midfielders and/or the defenders appear there. That was what happened in the second goal on Wednesday, with Sahin shooting almost inside the six-yard box. This needs a very good tactic work to avoid letting the team exposed to counterattack.

Finally, other option is to take advantage of the good shooting positions from distance that the team frequently gets as a result of exchanging passes near the box. I think that LFC could possibly draw more benefits than they are drawing now if they shot more often from distance.

Needless to say, all this approaches can, and should, be combined to effectively attack the opposition teams, and try and create more goal chances, which in turn will hopefully end up in more goals. There is individual and collective room for improvement. But the players seem to be enjoying the challenge, and improving slowly but steadily. And, amongst all the good news of this week is the feeling that the squad might be deeper than what many, myself included, feared. Well, not that a single game can prove anything, but it was a good indication.

As for the individual performances, my assessment would be that in the game against West Brom Jones, Wisdom, Coates, Robinson, Henderson, and Yesil did OK, without enhancing or damaging his first team chances; Carragher, Sahin, Pacheco and Assaidi did better than OK, improving their chances to be taking into account for the first team.

And Downing was very disappointing, not gaining any ground in his struggle to regain first team status.

One final special mention to the second goal, which probably epitomized what Rodgers wants for his team. The final action, Suso-Assaidi-Sahin was a joy to watch. But the previous action, with the exchanging of passes in the right wing, with the football finally getting to a clear zone before arriving to Suso, was a masterpiece of football craft.

All this said, the Norwich game can be a pivotal moment of the season. Hopefully next, and future, weeks will build on achievements of this one, to get the season on track.

5.- Luck, history, balance

Date: 2/10/2012
Previous matches: Norwich 2-5 LFC (Premier League)

As I wrote this (October 2nd) we are "celebrating" the 44th anniversary of one of the many times the luck has played its part in LFC history. That time it was for the worse for LFC: after winning 2-1 the second leg of the first round of the UEFA Cup against Athletic Club Bilbao, the accumulate result was a 3-3 draw and a coin (not a penalty shoot-out at the time) was to decide which team was going to progress. Ultimately, the coin ruled in favour of Athletic Club and LFC were knocked out.

Indisputably, that was luck in action. Regardless of what had happened during the matches, no player or manager had anything to do to influx the coin, so it was a case of sit and wait for the result. So, luck might sometimes play a part in football. But not always so indisputably. Precisely the introduction of the penalty shoot-out was a way to try and limit the part of the luck in the decision in the case of draws. And, while it is often said that penalty shoot-out are a matter of sheer luck, there is football ability involved to a certain extent. Partly luck, but not totally as in the case of the coin.

More difficult is to determine the importance of luck in football matches. A ball hitting woodwork (something we LFC supporters are experts in last seasons), bad luck or lack of accuracy?; decisive mistake by the opposition goalkeeper, good luck or lack of ability?; a football bouncing on a rival and going into the net, good luck or poor positioning of the rival?; well, any football fan can think of handfuls of other examples.

I have elsewhere discussed some of these points. But the Norwich game left me with another type of "luck consideration". That idea that over a season good and bad luck balance themselves, as presumably do good and bad refereeing decisions. I honestly have to admit that I tend to implicitly accept that point of view some times. So, any time LFC get a goal against in injury time (is it bad luck?) I almost at once consider that in the more or less near future LFC will likewise score in injury time (is it good luck?).

And lots of public statements by football related people insist time and again on that idea of a kind of magical self-balance over the length of a whole season between good/bad luck, good/bad refereeing decision, results deserved/undeserved, total points tally, and so on. However, the experience tells us that the theory doesn't really work. LFC don't need to go far back in time to realise it. Last season LFC's level of play deserved more points than achieved. And probably some other Premier League teams, too. (Needless to say, the concept of "deserved" points is a completely different issue, the football justice, maybe worth another post; anyway, football fans know what that means).

So, what about the Norwich match? Am I someway implying that LFC did not deserve that victory? Well, obviously not. LFC were the better team, and Suarez was absolutely unplayable for the Norwich defenders. What I am thinking is that in that automatic self-balance, LFC probably got a couple more goals than deserved last Saturday while in the match against ManU they probably got a couple less goals than deserved (maybe one for and one against). So, in a sense, the balance worked well. But in terms of points, it didn't. LFC deserved maybe a 2-1 victory against ManU and a 3-2 victory against Norwich, with six points in the table. But what was achieved was the same number of goal difference (+2) but only three points in the table.

My point being that there is no such balance; some times the luck plays in favour, some times plays against, but there is no overall compensation; and, even when one team has more or less certain actions in favour that somewhat compensate other actions than went against, the balance is very complicated to adequately reflect the sense of justice of the fans.

Hence, it is more useful to focus in the matches and how they went to draw the correct lessons for the team to progress. In that sense, it is important not to be too carried away by the 5-2 win against Norwich. LFC have played much better matches this season with less reward. During long spells of the first half, with the result still undecided, LFC were not in control of the game, with the midfielders suffering to cope with press and aggression of Norwich players. When in possession, the passes didn't quit go as fluidly as in other occasions.

That is not to say that bad news were more important that good news on the match. It is a huge relief to have grabbed the first league victory, and to have found the way towards the opposition goal. The team managed to handle a not easy match and run out comfortable winners, and that is a valuable asset to add to resources of the squad.

Individually, Wisdom had an encouraging match, and looked composed and firm with and without the ball; Suso was great assuring the circulation of the ball, and looked almost as an experienced player; Sahin and Allen played fairly well each one, but not as well as a pair, as they have still to find their game playing together, hopefully a matter of calendar time and pitch time; Gerrard had a good game, supporting both the midfield and the attack, and choosing wisely when to attack; Suarez was unstoppable, and can consider himself unlucky not to have scored more goals; on the other hand, Sterling had a poor match, with the odd brilliance but unable to really impose his game; and Reina looked quite unsecure.

As a whole, the team managed to inflict damage on a weak defence, which is very good news, but they were not really great in attack. And in defence (not specifically the defenders) the team still looks weak, conceding easy goals. The attacking side of the game seems to be adjusting and improving; the defensive side shows a lot of room for improvement and work needs to be done on training pitch. Conceding two goals nearly every match is something that needs to be addressed and fixed.

All in all, the team seems to be on the right track forward, but not quite there at the moment. But the path will be much more pleasant if victories keep coming in the process. And in that process the luck will undoubtedly go sometimes in favour and sometimes against; the team should focus on keep the path forward as designed. Incidentally, on that 1968/1969 UEFA Cup, Athletic Club went on and were knocked out by Glasgow Rangers on a controversial quarter final, in which the luck was on Rangers side. Maybe balancing that coin against LFC?

6.- Depth and width

Date: 11/10/12
Previous matches: LFC 2-3 Udinese (Uefa Europa League); LFC 0-0 Stoke (Premier League)

Under the guidance of Brendan Rodgers, LFC have quickly improved the circulation of the ball, the possession and the dominance of the games. Nothing happens now on the pitch without the knowing of LFC players. Still, the results are not quite as good as the team hope for. Last two games, 3-2 defeat against Udinese in Europa League and 0-0 against Stoke in Premier League, both in Anfield, have brought some doubts and unrest to LFC fans.

Different as they were, both matches had certain traits in common, and provide some food for thought. First obvious difference, of course, is the almost complete change in the players between the matches. Only Reina, Johnson and Allen started both games (and Johnson in opposite wings); then Suarez, Gerrard, Sterling, and Assaidi played some part as substitutes. In that respect, it may be somewhat irrelevant to try and draw common conclusions from those games, given that in fact they were played by different sets of players.

Well, somewhat; however, not completely irrelevant. The same fact of different players putting in practice Rodgers' ideas might be useful to have some insight in those ideas, the fundamentals that Rodgers like to see irrespective of the precise executants. In that sense, Europa League matches offer a valuable occasion to have a look at the development of the team. And indeed some conclusions about where the team is as of now can be drawn. Needless to say, conclusions based only on a couple of games have almost no statistical value at all, and can only be seen as indications of what might be happening and problems that may need to be addressed.

But anyway it is good material to discuss football. And for me the basic outcome of the matches is the insufficiency of collective attacking. This is not an isolate feature, but something the team have been showing since the start of the season, and it is proving to be difficult to fix. Generally speaking, the defensive mistakes tend to be individual, and attacking mistakes tend to be collective; correlatively, the team seems to be, slowly but steadily, adjusting in defence automatisms, and attacking well through individual actions.

Theoretically, a team needs either depth (towards the opposite goal) or width (using the wings), or in the best scenario both, to attack effectively as a collective from possession of the football. LFC are struggling to find both depth and width; as a result, the attack seems to be easy to defend by a strong defensive team which is firmly standing in its own half, sitting back and waiting for the rivals (LFC in this case) to come at them. And there are few teams as defensively strong as Stoke. As has been pointed out, this 0-0 has not been the first in Anfield against Stoke in last seasons. So it was always going to be a tough test for the attacking side of the team.

A tough test that, on this occasion, the team failed. The players couldn't find the wings, and seldom found the opposite box with clear chances. Barring a couple of potentially costing defensive mistakes that, for once, did not become goals this time, Stoke had hardly anything to say in LFC half. And the football was almost at any moment at the feet of LFC players. That said, they struggled to make that possession count, and couldn't find the way to Stoke box. One long distance shot by Gerrard; one personal action by Suarez, taking the ball from midfield until almost scoring the goal; one late cross which Skrtel was very close to converting in goal. And that is about everything on the attacking front. Not really enough to claim to have deserved the victory.

Not only the team did not find how to be deep, threatening the opposition box; the players could not find the wings, either. With Suso on one wing Rodgers gets a very good technician, a very useful link up player to give fluidity to the football; but loses a winger, unless clear instructions are given otherwise. On the other wing, Sterling seems to be looking for the inside areas of the pitch more often than proper wings. The usual remedy for this is the use of the full backs; but, as of now, Wisdom is a centre-back, not a full back, and cannot offer width in attack on a regular basis; and Johnson, a great full back, is really a right, not left, back. On the left he tries to add to the team, but cannot do it with the same ability and frequency as on the right.

Against Stoke, Suarez was the only player to offer real attacking aggression, the only one desperately trying to add that extra dimension of depth. It might have worked, but this time it didn't. More help is needed here, more players with that instinct of aiming at damaging more directly the opposition defence.

Some things had been a little bit better a few days earlier against Udinese. On the width front, Downing did his bit to provide much needed space and ability on the wing, causing all sorts of problems to the opposite defence. On the depth front, Shelvey added edge to the midfield, and the team looked, particularly during the first half, sharper. Even so, the capacity to transform the managing of the football and the rhythm of the match into clear chances should be much better, and in the second half the team lost its way and clarity. But some width and depth, even if not enough, was found by the team, more at least than days later against Stoke, showing an indication of where to work.

On the other hand, the defensive side of the team was much better on Sunday; against Udinese in the second half it was extremely frustrating to see the team concede not less than three goals against an opposition which not in its wildest dreams could have thought of scoring even one goal.

So, better in defence on Sunday; better in attack on Thursday. And clear fields to work on to keep improving. Even so, there is certain room for optimism. The team is progressing, though at a slower pace than we the fans would like. But at least Rodgers appears to have a clear vision of where he is trying to go. Time will tell the extent to which he obtains his goals.

Finally, there is another sense of depth in which Rodgers and the team are exceeding all expectations, namely the squad depth. The cup games are revealing a very valid set of players that could be of help for the first team, and might be valuable during the season. Improving the team spirit, having more players involved in the matches, can only be good news for the team. Hopefully Rodgers and the players will little by little find how to be wider, deeper, and ultimately better in front of goal.

7.- Up and coming

Date: 17/10/12
Previous matches: LFC U18 3-0 Middlesbrough U18 (U18 League)

One of the most mentioned features in Rodgers' tenure at LFC is that of his willingness to give the home-grown youngsters a shot in the first team, irrespective of their age, whenever the manager sees it fit for the team. And rightly so, after seeing Wisdom, Suso and Sterling repeatedly appearing in the first team.

Now, besides the understandable pride of the fans to see them on the pitch, sometimes the point is missed. There is a very thin line between the "if he is good enough, he is old enough" and the "as he is young enough, he is surely good enough". Getting the youngsters into the team is a tricky process that must be handled with care to ensure the best long term development. In that sense, it is not easy to know if the shortage of players, and the injuries that are speeding up the process will prove to be a blessing in disguise or an ultimate curse.

As of now, these two weeks without Premier games are probably a blessing, providing a much needed pause for reflection and thought inside the club. After his scintillating appearance in the first matches, Sterling certainly needed a pause to help grow his game. Suso was getting better by the day, and will probably use this pause to add to his game. Both are likely to be important players for the season. I am not so sure in the case of Wisdom; he has served the team well when needed, but he is not a natural full back, and may need more time to adapt.

Anyway, there can be little doubt that home-grown talent is key to LFC future, and even present. And that for whatever reason last years have not been fruitful on that front. The 90's gave about their fair share of players in Fowler, McManaman, Owen, Gerrard, Carragher; real first-class players. One can only dream of what could have been accomplished if it would have been possible to build a team around them all. But it wasn't to be. And no player that size has emerged from the Academy since then.

There have been good players, useful squad players, but not top-class. Now, the Wisdoms, Susos, and Sterlings are carrying the flame and may become what the team needs on that front; or maybe other U21 players that are around the first team. This season will probably be key for some of them in terms of showing their potential. Many of them have been playing together under Rodolfo Borrell for two or three years, being a very good team in their age groups. Now they have ahead of them the most difficult step in their developing, becoming senior top players.

LFC and Brendan Rodgers will need them to step up and contribute to the first team not only in this very season, but in the following ones. There is no sustainable (maybe nor desirable) way at this moment for LFC to build a team buying every player. And in his first months in charge Rodgers has proven, if anything, that he is keen to give the young players a chance.

Further down the ranks, there is an U18 team that looks very promising, too. I only have had the chance to see them in one complete match, their 3-0 victory against Middlesbrough U18 a couple of weeks ago. I didn't have the chance to write then, but I have remained under the impression that the current U18 are a very good team, with some extremely promising prospects that hopefully will be able to keep adding to first squad in years to come. If the Academy manages to keep producing teams capable of consistently feeding the senior of squad with two/three players each age group, that will be a great path to building a successful team.

Watching this U18 team demolish Middlesbrough I couldn't help but recalling that team that forms now the core of the U21 team. Before I go on, I want to stress that I have only seen them in one full match, and some highlights of other matches; meaning that I openly admit that all the judgements I am about to express might very well prove to be unfounded, once the season unfolds. But, for what is worth, here are my views.

The players seemed, first and foremost, a very good football team. They were very well placed on the pitch, they knew how and when to move to where they were most needed, both defending and attacking. They have probably worked very hard on the training ground, not only this season, but also in past ones. And Steve Cooper seems to be a very capable coach. The team absolutely bossed the match from the beginning, building from the holding of the football and taking it to the most dangerous areas of the pitch, while preventing the opposition from doing any harm.

Even if they were 3-0 already at half time (and consequently 0-0 in the second half), second half was as good, if not better, in the handling of the match. It could have easily finished 5-0 or 6-0. It was one of those days in which every player simply seemed on fire. Even the keeper Fulton looked very composed in the rare occasion in which he was called into action. Both full-backs, Quirk (right) and Maguire (left), were solid in defence and supported tirelessly the attack being, looking comfortable on the ball while, when needed, extremely profound and putting very good footballs into the opposite box. The two centre-backs, Jones and Heaton, had very few work to do in defence; even so, when they had to, they were great. When on the attack, both were good; Heaton looked particularly good when on the ball, assuring the transition to the midfielders or even the long ball when appropriate; a very impressing prospect. Jones was very good causing havoc in Middlesbrough defence, and only bad luck prevented him from scoring.

Playmakers Baio and Lussey made everything that one could expect from them. Baio looked physically imposing, but in all truth I think he was the "not so good" (I can not say the worse, he played fine) player on the day. Lussey was terrific; easily head and shoulders above every other player on the field. He played near the defenders, he approached the forwards, went form one flank to the other, set the rhythm for the game in every moment, scored a great goal, and overall bossed the match. A real joy to watch. That said, it is true that the rivals gave him acres of space in every moment; if he can replicate that kind of form repeatedly, and especially in front of different types of opposition, he would be a real gem. But in midfield that is difficult, and he will probably need more physical work; anyway, his footballing brain seems (or seemed at that particular match) fantastic.

On the wings, Peterson (right) and Gainford (left) were a constant threat. Gainford played probably a little bit better on the day, and showed some impressive skills. But both were real assets to the attacking side of the team, and knew how to cause problems to defenders. Behind the striker, Trickett-Smith looked lively, and impossible to read for the opposition. He constantly appeared where unexpected, and found how to be undetectable for the rivals, while linking well with the midfielders and the wings. As a striker, Sinclair showed the kinds of qualities that have made him the youngest player ever on the first team, always with an eye on goal and finding space.

Overall, a very good display. Again, one match is not nearly enough to make a definite judgement, and coming matches will confirm, or refute, these early impressions. At these ages, many players seem to be better than they get years after, and in the best case these players are some seasons away from become first team regulars, so no need to be over optimistic. Time to enjoy their games, particularly if they keep coming this way. As for Rodgers and the near future, the fringe players and the U21 squad are way more important.

8.- Ambition, realism

Date: 24/10/12
Previous matches: LFC 1-0 Reading (Premier League)

It is sometimes said that one of the traits (not the only, of course) of a really successful team, company, person, you name it, is that they are never satisfied with what they have got, they are always aiming higher. If that is really the case, I might well be on my way to success...as a football fan. I mean, LFC won its last game, kept a second consecutive league clean sheet, started to climb the table,...From that perspective, the Reading game might be considered a success to a great extent.

But I am not happy with the game. I am obviously fine with the victory, and with the clean sheet. But not with how it was achieved. Needless to say, I have no insight at all on the decision making process that led to the specific game plan. It might very well be good reasons behind the choices made. But from what I know (merely as an spectator) I think that what I saw was a slight step back from what Rodgers has been trying to instil in the team since last summer.

For the first time, the team opted consistently in defence to give time and space to opposition players after losing the ball, waiting in own half. And, when in attack, players looked time and again for quick transitions and tried to reach the opposition box with few passes, with far more long balls in that single game than in any of the previous ones.

Now, there is nothing particularly wrong with that approach. A successful team can apply it, and indeed some do. However, it somewhat contradicts with what Rodgers have been doing until now. I will summarize my concerns in three points. Two of them footballistic, one of them purely personal. On the football front, the new plan didn't really work on Saturday. Even if the rivals were one of the weakest teams in the Premier, the game was never under LFC control, much less in the second half, so the final result was always in doubt.

In attack, LFC kept relying almost exclusively on Luis Suarez, who was fantastic in every front except actually scoring. The support came from Sterling at times, and more consistently from Johnson, who played one of his better games as left-back, being a constant threat and unfortunate not to score. Some good chances appeared, but not as much and as clear as one might expect playing at Anfield against such opposition.

Defensively, Reading looked always a credible threat, a goal against LFC never too far. Jones made some good saves, and the football was around his box more often than desired. It was not a case of a team controlling the game without the ball; it was a case of a game never really controlled by LFC, with the midfield too often in troubles. Suarez, Sterling and Suso work as much as they are asked to. But, as of now, there are not enough automatisms in place for them to help the midfield when the football is missed for long spells; and in such occasions, Allen, Gerrard and Sahin cannot cover all the midfield by themselves, and as a result the team loses control of the action.

The second footballing concern for me is that the team was up to this game on a learning curve of what Rodgers wanted of them; if they are going to play differently now, they could end up being confused, and not playing well one way nor the other. That has happened a lot in world football, so hopefully it is simply a case of either a bad day at the office or some circumstances leading the staff to make adjustments. In this sense, the fact that many of the players played international games in midweek and thus conceivable being not fully fit may have something to do with it.

The purely personal concern is simply that I very much prefer my team to be dominating the games, dictating the rhythm, and being proactive, than waiting for the rivals to make mistakes and being reactive. But I can totally see that a team can be successful either way, so this is not really relevant.

Up until now, it may look that I was not only disappointed, but even depressed, after the game, and that I found everything negative. Not at all. There were many positives also, and a victory was extremely needed, and thus important on that day. Amongst the positives, Johnson, who played very well as a left-back, being a constant threat to opposition and a constant help to LFC attack. Still, I cannot help thinking that he might have been even better as a right-back.

The match Suarez played was simply outstanding. Even more so, given his week with Uruguay. He was almost anywhere on the pitch, tormenting the defenders, helping his team-mates, and being close to scoring time and again. He deserved to score after playing so well. Sterling had very good moments, along with other ones not so good. But his first goal will no doubt help his progress and boost his confidence.

As for the style of play, I have expressed my concern over the lack of control by LFC midfielders, with constant turnovers; but it is very true that the team needed to add more verticality and use the football possession and passes with more edge, inflicting more damage to the rival defenders. And the Reading game might have been a good experiment in that direction, adding more football weapons to use in coming matches if and when needed. Having more tactics in the repertoire can only improve the level of the team and squad.

Overall, LFC were by far the better team and ran out deserved winners. Some evolution was seen on the play of the team. And my concerns are after all only a sign of how highly I rate the potential of the team and my expectations as LFC fan, not only in terms of results but also in terms of level of play and game dominance. That said, a win and a clean sheet are realistically good achievements in a process of building a team, if combined with the proper ambition to keep building and improving.

9.- A match with a bit of everything

Date: 30/10/2012
Previous matches: Everton 2-2 LFC (Premier League)

The match against Everton left a great deal of feelings, ideas, hopes, frustrations, and son on. On one hand, the result was not brilliant, not awful; on the other hand, the level of play was…not brilliant, not awful. Instead of some players playing well and some playing poorly, as it is usually the case, almost every player played…not brilliantly, not awfully.

Even more puzzling, the game was something of a rollercoaster. Not only the first half was completely different from the second half from LFC's point of view, but within both halves every ten or fifteen minutes everything changed, and one could go from expecting a wide margin victory to a wide margin defeat to a hardly fought draw. Five minutes from the final whistle and it was nearly impossible to decide if the sensible thing to do was to settle for a draw or to unreservedly go for a win.

So, many different matches in one, each one of them worth its own commenting and analysing. It is very difficult to reach a conclusion about the match as a whole. While it is true that LFC might (indeed, should) have run out winners with that final wrongly disallowed goal, it is equally true that there were some spells during the match in which Everton clearly outplayed LFC (and vice versa). In that sense, a draw might be seen as a fair result by both teams, but that is seldom the case, and each team may feel that they could have won the game.

Being impossible to comment on every aspect of the match, I would like to look mainly at the tactics put in place by LFC, the approach to the game, and the changes at halftime. That was, at least, interesting, and maybe even revealing of a certain evolution in Rodgers thoughts after these first few months of the season.

Since his appointment Rodgers kept talking, time and again, of his idea of playing football from the possession, using that possession both to prevent rivals from damaging his team and to make his team inflict damage on the opposition. While it was by no means the first time an LFC manager tried to instil that idea into the team, it appeared to be particularly important for him, and his key goal for the football year.

For the first games of the season it was there to be seen how the team tried hard to keep hold of the football, to play from the possession. It was a learning process and sometimes the players played better than other times; but the idea was clear. The goalkeeper almost always playing short balls, the defenders trying to reach the midfielders, and the midfielders circulating the ball around looking for a good opportunity to arise and get the ball forward. However, the results were not always as good as expected, or even deserved. The team was apparently progressing, but maybe too slowly. Or maybe Rodgers considered that the possession aspect had been to an extent achieved, and other aspects needed to be added, both in attack and in defence.

Anyway, a couple of games ago things started to change, and the team began to play more long balls and focus less in keeping the football. They started to pay more attention to counterattacks and keeping the defence structure ready, defending closer to the own box. Those changes were particularly seen in the Reading game. And an evolution of it was seen on the Everton game.

In football it is never easy to say to what extent a team is doing what they want to do, or what the rivals force them to do. But against Everton, LFC was unable to keep possession of the ball, and opted for either long balls or quick transitions to attack, with way fewer passes than at the beginning of the season. Allen, Gerrard, Sahin, with the help of Suso, were, somewhat predictably, unable to cope with the physical strength of the Everton midfielders. Less predictable was that they were also unable to keep the ball moving, of exchanging passes between them, of keeping at least the possession. As a result, Agger and Skrtel found themselves in a difficult fight to keep the ball far from Jones' box, with the constant threat of the holes left behind when either of them moved up to chase the ball.

All that put in this way, it seems like a desperate situation for LFC. And it was not. At the same time, Suarez and Sterling, with the help of, again, Suso, and remarkably Enrique, were able to create all sorts of problem on the Everton half. Sometimes long balls; other times a quick succession of short balls, Everton defenders were caught repeatedly in problems.

It was this situation, with both teams able to ask questions from opposition defenders and struggling to properly answer the questions asked, that made the first half and absolute thriller that could have ended, say, 3-0 for LFC or 3-0 for Everton. Or 3-3. Or, as it was the case, 2-2. Although, in all truth, Everton were slightly better. It was a little bit frustrating for LFC that both goals conceded came after serious mistakes by LFC players; they might have arrived after good actions from Everton, but in fact they were the result of poor defending. Anyway, halftime and 2-2 was the score.

And then Rodgers had to decide. Keeping the things more or less the same was an obvious risk, given that Everton had ended the first time on top. But changing things the way he did was also a risk. Pondering both risks, he decided to act and try to solve the problems. With Coates he added more aerial power and more cover for the now three central defenders to go after the ball knowing that two defenders remained behind. With Shelvey he added a more powerful, more box-to-box midfielder, strong in the middle and able to help the attack, with Gerrard higher up on the pitch, supporting Sterling and Suarez. For Everton defenders, having two strikers to take care of made it more difficult for them to support the midfield.

Obviously, every gain comes at a cost. On the minus side, losing Suso and Sahin meant less ball control, less capacity to dictate the rhythm of the match, and subjecting the tactics to counteract the strengths of the opposition and not to enhance the own strengths. Both aspects were seen on the pitch. For both sides it became much more difficult to damage the opposition. LFC improved with Henderson, who was a real threat from the right flank, the way Enrique had been in the first half from the left flank. But it was not enough to unbalance the score; well, or maybe it was just enough, but that goal did not count.

It is almost a philosophical question if it is a good idea to make those changes not only from game to game, but even in the middle of a game. There are setbacks to it, but LFC fans have in our memory certain May 25th 2005 in which a halftime substitution, a midfielder (Hamann) for a right back (Finnan) absolutely changed the game to a good end. More important that playing with two or three centre-backs is to clarify if the possession will remain the way to control the games, or if the team will try another approach. Time will tell.

Time will tell, also, whether Rodgers is changing his initial ideas or completing the repertoire of the team, trying to get ready to face the different challenges that the season will keep posing. Whether he has given up playing from the possession or trying to get his squad ready for confronting all kinds of opposition teams. Whether this season will be a good one, a poor one, or…not brilliant, not awful.

10.- Where football is

Date: 03/11/12
Previous matches: LFC U18 4-2 Wolves U18 (U18 League)

In one of the "Tracks" he released in 1998, Bruce Springsteen sang that he wanted to "be where the bands are". In these early days of 12/13 season, an LFC fan that wants to be where the football is should be watching the matches of U18 team. Not that it is by any means a perfect team, as can be seen by the table standings. They have won, but also lost and drawn. But they know how to play, and almost always they play entertaining and quality matches.

They try to play a similar style of play as the first team try. But I tend to think that, while both teams are learning that style of play, U18 players are more advanced in their learning curve. They look more comfortable in it, that way of playing looks more natural for them. For example, one aspect that is turning out to be difficult for first team defenders (and goalkeeper) is to keep hold of the ball and pass it in good condition to the midfielders. In the match against Wolves they confronted a team which pressed high up on the pitch, putting a great deal of pressure on the defenders. As Springsteen sang in other of the "Tracks", a situation in which "a good man is hard to find" ("a good man" being, obviously, a team mate).

In those circumstances, the outcome of the situation was not always ideal, but was always to an extent controlled.

The team tried to keep possession and pass the ball around looking for a chance to come forward to appear. All four defenders, and the keeper, seemed confident in the process. Sometimes, as Wolves players were so advanced on the pitch, LFC players found spaces behind Wolves' midfielders and could make a quick transition to dangerous positions in attack; sometimes the ball simply arrived at the foot of LFC midfielders to build a positional attack.

However, in other occasions the pressure was too good (or LFC players too weak) and the ball was lost, or at least the threat was there. What I found remarkable in those occasions was that LFC players were never caught out of position. Sometimes, they kicked hopeless long balls that gave them time to recover position; sometimes, they carried the ball to a flank in which the loss was less dangerous. In that sense, they limited their losses brilliantly. Even when giving away the ball, at least there was no clear chance for the opposition as a result.

I think that is something the first time is still to achieve. And it is probably at least partially behind the decision to play much more long balls than in the first matches of the season. Anyway, that is something Rodgers no doubt would like his players to perform. In attack there are, as of now, more differences between the U18 and the first team. The extent to which those differences are due to the teams being a work in construction or to differences in the approach of the managers, is not clear at the moment.

U18 players tend to attack much more flowingly than the first team, and with much more players supporting the attack. Almost every player, except the centre-backs (and even they, depending on the moment), gets into attacking positions to offer options to the player in possession. As a result, the player on the ball has usually several options to choose from. That said, they seldom concede clear counterattacks to the rivals.

Both aspects in which the team manages not to concede clear chances (after losing the ball in defence, or finishing the attack) talks of a great positional play. The players know where they need to go on the pitch to maximize their positive impact and minimize the negative. At any given moment, all the playing pitch is adequately covered by LFC players. That is instrumental if a team wants to play from the possession of the ball. If the positional aspects are not well worked on, the possession tends to cause the players to lose position and ultimately leads to big spaces that the opposition might take advantage of. Playing from the possession needs to come along with good positional play.

When a team is capable of keeping a good structure while attacking with the ball as well as while defending, that provides good foundations to build on. There is where U18 are. There is where football is. From there, U18 players use the wings much more than the first team. Maybe it is the managers' ideas; maybe it is that there are players capable of that. The use of the wings is very clever, with players going in and out, making it difficult for the opposition defenders to read the movements. At the same time, the central players know when and how to get to the box to make the most of it.

It might be thought that everything is perfect and rosy in the team. Clearly, it is not. Team and players are learning, and targets are not always achieved. Against Wolves, in a 4-2 win, LFC have had both, good and not so good moments. The beginning of the match was great, with a first goal around ten minutes and a penalty loss at fifteen minutes. But after twenty, or twenty-five, very good minutes, the team started to struggle. For some reason, finding that "good man" became increasingly difficult, and Wolves were more and more around LFC box, and had good chances to score.

Just before half-time, a penalty against LFC led to a well deserved draw. It was in a sense bad luck for Felton, LFC goalkeeper. He made an outstanding save from penalty shot, only to see the follow-up go into the net, in part maybe (it is difficult to be sure) because a lack of attention by defenders. After half-time, LFC came back to good moments, and scored a couple of goals to put the score at 3-1. Then there were some difficult moments, similar to those in the first half, but although the team conceded the 3-2, LFC were able to navigate the match better in the second half than in the first. To finish on a high, Sinclair scored a wonderful goal; not spectacular, maybe, but full of ability and displaying plenty of striker qualities. Great goal.

All in all, an irregular match, with very good spells and other not so good. But the structure was there, the foundations were there, to support the team in the worse moments. The centre-backs were solid both on and off the ball. The full-backs were good in defence, but perhaps not so prolific in attack. Probably many difficulties were caused by the indifferent game by the most influential player, the captain Lussey, who for one reason or another was not at his best (even so, he was at times very good). Likewise, Trickett-Smith, usually instrumental in the control of the game from his position behind the striker, was not at his best, either. To compensate those setbacks, Baio as a holding midfielder, and Peterson and Ojo on the wings were excellent, causing all sorts of problems to the opposition defenders. In the box, Sinclair did what he does best, finalising by putting the ball into the net.

So, yes, as of now, LFC U18 team is where football is. Even when not playing at their best, as was the case against Wolves, the team offers good things, and good football. Definitely, this team is "growin' up" (by the way, another Springsteen's Track). Hopefully they will keep progressing.

11.- The Audacity of Hope

Date: 07/11/12
Previous matches: LFC 1-1 Newcastle (Premier League);
Wolves U21 1-5 LFC U21 (U21 League)

Some years ago, while still a candidate, Barack Obama published his second book, "The Audacity of Hope". Since I am writing this shortly after his re-election as President of the U.S.A., I felt it fit to use it as the key concept of the post. Well, not only that; also, it kind of summarizes the ambivalence of the current state of affairs in LFC.

In two different ways: for the worse because it takes audacity, as of now, to have hope in the team, given the way in which it is performing lately; for the better, the phrase focus on the positive aspects of hope, and the potential rewards of having that audacity. After the Newcastle game, I admit I was left with little, if any, hope. I am aware that some pundits, as well as LFC players and manager, have stressed the positives of the match, and some undeniably hopeful actions and consequences that can be dragged from it. The first twenty minutes, the performances of Enrique and Suarez or the unbelievable goal made between them, to name a few.

But I confess that I felt the negatives were of far more significance. One more time, the team was unable to capitalise on the Anfield factor; as of now, LFC is, if I am not mistaken, the worst team in points won at home during 2012. Even if it is not the worst, but one of the worst, it is not acceptable (though, of course, only a part of it have been during Rodgers tenure). One more time, the team conceded in one of the very, very, few chances of the opposition team. There is a good side of that: few chances allowed; and a bad side: it takes very little for a rival to score against LFC. One more time, LFC was unable to turn its huge possession rate into good scoring chances. That is very worrying, I think.

And it is something in which no improvement is being seen. Time and again, LFC tries, and usually, success in, having the possession more time than the opposition; and time and again that possession turns out to be fruitless in terms of getting good positions to score. Many LFC goals end up coming from counterattacks and/or long passes, and very few from open play and long possessions. Obviously, turning possession into chances is not an easy task. But it is imperative if the team is going places this season. In all truth, playing exactly the same LFC could have won the match; it was possibly what was deserved, even. But more authority is badly needed in these types of matches, putting the result beyond doubt.

I was thinking along these lines, trying to figure out what to write about the match; and to make things worse, I received a message from a friend (huge LFC fan) saying in similar mood that better not to talk about the team. So I was focusing on the need to find the audacity when it come the rescue. Not for the first time, the U21s (formerly the reserves, formerly the U18s) of Rodolfo Borrell were there to emphatically reinforce the hope with their 5-1 away victory against Wolves.

A 5-1 that came after a rather flat first half in which Wolves took the lead shortly before half-time. But somehow the team turned a performance full of good intentions but not of good outcomes during the first half into a storm of goals during the second half. If I was looking for hope (and I was, though unconsciously), hope I got. The team was unstoppable in that second half. Sometimes it only takes one fine adjustment to make everything click; this time, it was the introduction of Teixeira for Yesil at half-time. Not that Yesil played particularly worse than his team-mates in the first half; not that Teixeira played particularly better than them in the second half. But there appeared that click that triggered a dramatic improvement in the effectiveness of the team.

Borrell made an audacious move: instead of moving Ngoo up front, he was kept on the right and, with Teixeira on the left and Adorjan on the hole, Pacheco played as a striker. A non-conventional striker that made the team unplayable. Pacheco moved along the attack, left, right and centre; Ngoo and Teixeira were very clever in supporting him where more harm could be done, sometimes on the wings, sometimes on the inside. And, of course, there was also the necessary bit of luck, in the form of early goals. Should the equaliser have taken longer to come, the result, the performance, the hope, could have been completely different.

But goals came, and in that second half the team managed to play extraordinarily well and take advantage of the circumstances of the match. Pacheco looked head and shoulders above every other player on the pitch, scoring seemingly at will. Teixeira did not seem to be playing his first (or almost his first) competitive match with his teammates. It seemed that he had been playing there for ages. Ngoo looked like a man playing with children each and every time he faced the rivals. Adorjan was always there to provide to precise assistance, the accurate pass. Roddan and Pelosi, on the midfield, and the defenders, did what was needed from them: stop the opposition and carry the football as quickly as possible to the forwards.

True that all of these came after a much less impressing first half, so things should obviously be put in perspective. This U21 team is far from being the finalised article. But in a time LFC needed an injection of hope, they performed that great second half. Good for them. Most difficult is to know if there were any lessons or direct help for the first team. Being a good team, Wolves U21 are nothing like the usual rivals the first team has to confront, and a similar performance would be much more difficult in the Premier League. Still, some consequences might be possible.

The type of play needed to get into scoring positions with mobile players instead of a towering striker is what the U21 played. And one of the things that is not working as of now is the role of Sahin behind Suarez. Sahin is a great player, but he is used to playing in a role more similar to what Allen is playing now. Either he quickly learns the keys to his new role or another player will have to play there; within the first team Gerrard, Shelvey and Suso could fill that position, or maybe Pacheco could be given a chance. Besides that, the attitude and type of play of Ngoo could be of use. He is a player capable of the best and of the worst; he can be frustrating at times. But he adds to the team the edge and ambition to always try to create problems to defenders. Something Sterling does sometimes, and Suso does not, simply because he is a different type of player, that does other things for the benefit of the team. Maybe a certain controlled dose of Ngoo could be helpful at certain games.

Anyway, from Monday afternoon I look at the team with a different and stronger audacity and hope, thanks partially to that second half. Let's wait and see what next term has for President Obama and what comes for LFC against Anzhi and Chelsea in coming matches.

12.- Versatility, confusion

Date: 16/11/12
Previous matches: Chelsea 1-1 LFC (Premier League)

Generally speaking, in life versatility is a good thing; confusion is a bad one. Football is no different in that. Of course one could find exceptions; but, in general terms, it is good to have versatility on your side, the dark side of it being confusion. As of now, I am afraid LFC and Brendan Rodgers are closer to confusion than to versatility.

Against Chelsea Rodgers tried yet another system and different tactics. And frankly, I do not think it worked. Admittedly, result was good enough. Moreover, it could have been even better, with those last chances Suarez and Enrique had. But it was not a good match, by either team. And hopefully a good result is not going to disguise that fact. LFC should aspire to better performances, to more capability of creating chances, of stamping its authority on a match, of dictating longer spells of the match.

However, it is true that new systems and new tactics demand from a team time to adjust to them. So it might be the case that Rodgers is adding versatility to the team and, in time, that work will pay off in terms of a more capable set of players and a more adaptable team. But for the time being the players look more confused than progressing.

Regarding the system, Rodgers started playing 4-3-3 in every match, and explaining its virtues and how he wanted his team to play that way; in the last matches, the team has been deployed on 5-3-2, 4-2-3-1, and 3-4-3, apart from the 4-3-3. As stated, versatility in itself is not by any means a bad trait for a football team. But if it leads to confusion, it could have bad effects on the players. The roles of players involved are different, and the players may need to adjust their game. One particular victim of all these changes seems to be Allen, who looks increasingly confused.

Sometimes he plays alongside Gerrard with two centre-backs at their backs; sometime he plays as only holding midfielder; sometimes, as playmaker; sometimes, alongside Shelvey; sometimes, in front of three centre-backs, or almost alongside Coates; and, on last Sunday, alongside Sahin. While Allen is surely more than able to interpret each of these parts in the team, it would be almost supernatural from him to deliver all the parts in just few weeks. At least, to deliver at the high standards we all, and I am sure he himself, expects from him. More so given that he has just arrived in a legendary club.

As a result, he works more and more to less and less outcomes. And, he being the cornerstone of the team, it has a direct effect on his team-mates. Gerrard is not looking any comfortable of late. And Sahin is not the shadow of the player he was at Germany. Midfield is the key to the game Rodgers wants to play, and it is not working. It seems as if Rodgers himself is still getting to know his players and their capabilities.

And it seems as if Rodgers is coming to the conclusion that his players are not capable of playing the way he would like them to play. And he is trying to find a way suitable to the players. Again, this coin has two faces: it is a good thing to try and find a way to play that allows the players to play to the best of their qualities; on the other hand, doing it in a hurry, with seemingly not enough time of work on training pitch, pressed by the results, is not a good thing.

Rodgers is not only changing the system, he is also changing the tactics. Sometimes the goal is to have the ball, keep the possession, and try to dominate the game from there. Sometimes the goal is to be on the opposition half as soon as possible, with long balls; sometimes the transition defence-attack is slow with a large number of passes; sometimes the team wants to achieve the box in a few passes. Sometimes the defence is high up the pitch, near the opposition box; sometimes the team sits back to protect the own box; sometimes the attitude is to try and get back the football as soon as possible; sometimes, only to watch and prevent the rivals from getting into scoring positions.

This is difficult for the players, and they have not much time to work on it on the training ground. Even so, as said, all good if it is versatility; all worrying if it is confusion. And now, if feels more as confusion to me. Needless to say, there are also good signs. LFC is now six league games without conceding defeat, which may provide a good platform to improve. Although Chelsea was the better team last Sunday, it was not great superiority, and LFC achieved an acceptable result.

As to individual performances, Suso really made the difference when on the pitch, adding almost the only source of verticality and ambition to the team. Without him, it is difficult to see how could have the team achieved even the draw. Also, the near telepathic understanding between Jose Enrique and Suarez may become a great weapon in matches to come. Finally, Carragher giving an assist might indeed be confusing, but involves no doubt a very welcome versatility.

13.- Calmed victory

Date: 21/11/12
Previous matches: LFC 3-0 Wigan (Premier League)

For way too long, LFC has been waiting for a match in the shape of last Saturday's against Wigan. Was it a brilliant match? Not exactly. Particularly well played? Not quite, really. The team was dominant, in charge of the match, and the goals ended up coming the LFC way. Sometimes a team needs these kinds of matches, in which they don't need to perform heroics to win.

It was a match LFC won by means of "simply" being a better team, with better players. It is something the dominant teams around are used to, but something that it is being elusive to LFC. Time and again, in last seasons, LFC have been drawing, or even losing, these games, especially at Anfield. LFC were not much better than Wigan, and did not play spectacularly well. But kept the game under control, dictated the rhythm of the match, and played near the opposition box.

Normally, that is enough to win games if your players are better than the rivals. And finally that happened at Anfield. Wigan almost never threatened Reina, who had a very quiet return to the Premier League. It provided a very welcome platform to build on. It is never easy to know to what extent it was because LFC's defensive system worked very well, or because Wigan attacking game was uninspired on the day. Surely it was helpful on that front that the team tried to press high up the pitch, and was much more aggressive in defending than during last matches.

Anyway, once the back was adequately covered, the team was able to focus on the attack. It was not particularly impressive. Once again, the team showed that adjustments are needed in the attacking side of the game. Allen is struggling to dictate the game, to ensure a correct transition of the football from defenders to midfielders and forwards. He works his shocks off game after game, and shows glimpses of his undeniable quality, but he was more inspired in his first games of the season. Maybe he is a little bit tired, maybe he is finding it difficult to settle, maybe he is finding it difficult to step up in a club like LFC and become the dominant force in midfield.

Gerrard is also looking somewhat confused; even so, he is one of the best players in the team, but he is not quit reaching his peak. He seems to be struggling to adjust his game to the role of helping Allen to build the game and getting in advanced positions to help the attack. In the process, he is caught sometimes out of position. Maybe all that is needed is for both of them, Allen and Gerrard, to work on the pitch together and adjust their playing to each other, and learn how to best play together.

The case of the third piece in midfield was interesting. From the beginning, and during the first half an hour, Suso was probably the best player on the pitch, playing in the hole behind Suarez. He was lively, he was skilful, he was dangerous. However, still in the first half Rodgers opted to replace him with Henderson, who played more inserted in midfield, allowing Gerrard and especially Enrique to advance their positions, to a good effect on the team.

Sometimes taking off the best players can have a positive impact on the team, rebalancing the players and resulting in fine tuning. I am not really sure if this was the case against Wigan. I don't have the impression that team played better as a whole after the substitution. However, it is clear that the goals came then, and that the more advanced role of Enrique played a part in it. It seems that the telepathic understanding between Enrique and Suarez keeps improving, and Rodgers' inspired decision to play Enrique higher up the pitch is possibly a fitting reaction to that.

Placing near on the ground players that understand well each other can only work for the benefit of the team, and Suarez and Enrique clearly enjoy playing with each other, and it shows on the pitch and on the score sheet. Apparently, all that was needed against Wigan was to keep the back secured, get the football close to Suarez and Enrique, and wait for the goals to come. Although, obviously enough, it is not near as easy as it sounds. To begin with, securing the back involves a great deal of hard work when not in possession.

Starting from the forwards, every player got involved in pressing, closing spaces, and getting the ball back. Which was epitomised in the probably decisive first goal; no doubt it was a mistake by Wigan defender. No doubt, either, Sterling fought for it and Suarez was ready to capitalise. But it was not the only time LFC players were ready to press. Only sometimes the pressing results in an almost direct goal, but in other occasions is also useful for the team in impeding the attacking play by the opposition, and making the life easier for LFC defenders.

At the end of the day, a very welcome calmed victory, that should allow the team to keep growing and adjusting. There is much room for improvement, particularly in the attacking side, in turning the possession of the football into clear goal chances. But being able to win matches in a controlled way is a good thing, and a sign of a mature team, although it should not disguise the need for that improvement to occur.

14.- Same eleven, worse result

Date: 29/11/12
Previous matches: LFC 1-3 Swansea (League Cup); Swansea 0-0 LFC (Premier League); Tottenham 2-1 LFC (Premier League)

In what is becoming an increasingly unusual decision, Rodgers decided to name the exact starting eleven in last two Premier League matches. Even more unusual given that both games were played in half a week. The balance cannot be positive, one draw and one defeat. There is room for analysis in the development of the matches and in that decision. What went right, what went wrong in those matches, what can be learned from them.

It is often said that if someone wants a different output, he should put in a different input. Changing causes would be, in this vision, the best way to change consequences. Accepting that approach, it might be the case that Rodgers liked what he saw in the Swansea game, and wanted a similar performance by the team. Although such approach is extremely dubious when it comes to football matches, where lots of unpredictable things can happen and affect the unfolding of the game, it might be worth it to accept that premise, just for a moment, and reflect on to what extent Swansea game should, or should not, be seen as a model for LFC.

Overall, I should start by making clear that I don't thing that Swansea game was particularly good. There were, true, good aspects in it; but it was not nearly what LFC should aspire at, in terms, obviously, of result; but in terms also of level of play. Good news was at the back, with Swansea attack almost completely nullified by LFC defensive system. Reina was little more than a spectator for almost the whole game. That is not little achievement against Swansea away, and Rodgers and players fully deserve recognition for that. It is a good sign for coming games if the team is able to keep that defensive form.

However, the attacking side of the team, even the controlling side of the team, was much less satisfactory. Some chances were created, and we may never know if Enrique was really offside when scoring. But, yet again, the team struggled to consistently impose its authority on the game, and to turn the dominant parts of the match into real spells of goal scoring threats. The team is still unable to attack as a whole, leaving everything to the odd individual brilliance or inspiration.

On the whole, there were an encouraging sign in the ambition of the players, the attitude of going for the match and not settling for a draw; but a disappointing sign in the lack of real authority on the game. An LFC team should give more; this time LFC could have been deserved winners, and if one team was to win the game, it should have been LFC. But the gap between the teams was narrow, and a draw is not totally unfair, really. The aim for LFC should be to be much more superior, and to get clear victories, at least from time to time.

Whatever the reason, Rodgers not only did not make all substitutions during Swansea match, but indeed kept the same team to confront Tottenham. In many ways, the game was similar, and the difference in the final result could be attributed to the difference in quality between Swansea and Tottenham; more specifically, to the fact that Gareth Bale plays for Tottenham. But there were some telling differences.

The almost rock-solid defence against Swansea was nowhere to be seen during the initial 25/30 minutes on Wednesday, in which LFC players, including Reina, gave all kinds of opportunities to Bale in particular and Tottenham attack in general. If that were the real level of LFC defence, there would be little to do over the season. On the other hand, it was somewhat remarkable the way in which things were pretty much fixed after those 30 minutes. It is really difficult to turn around performances in that way, but someway LFC players managed to do that. I must admit that, from the telly, I could not tell if there were any tactical changes at all in that front; but from the end of the first half, and through the second half, Tottenham was much less damaging in attack.

That improvement provided a fit base to build on, and the team grew on the pitch from that terrible start to the match. There were many difficulties, many mistakes, and apparent weaknesses; but the attacking side of the team and the dictating of the match by LFC players were better than against Swansea. More chances were created, though not enough to even draw the match. The team still finds it extraordinarily difficult to turn possession into chances, to find that final edge into opposition lines. However, the attacking was better on Wednesday than on Sunday, and it may be a good path to keep walking on in coming matches.

As of now, it seems that the player that can provide that edge is Shelvey. He is a player difficult to decipher, combining blatant mistakes with brilliant actions. But being difficult to decipher is not always a bad thing in an attacking player, and he adds to the team that goal-oriented mind that is needed. Three players gave particular food for thought over the two games. Enrique, playing in an unfamiliar advanced role, showed that he is capable of causing problems to opposition defenders, through his mobility, ambition, and work rate. He also showed that he is not the player a top team needs in that position, because of his lack of quality on the ball and his unreliable reading of the game. As an emergency solution, however, he might be useful on that role.

Johnson is a much, much better right-back than left-back. He is a waste on the left; not that he cannot do a job there, but he is much more useful on the right, particularly on the attack. It might be a good idea to try him on an advanced role, similar to that of Enrique, and see if he can perform there. Anyway, he is a constant threat while playing on the right, and only provides the odd threat while playing on the left. Finally, Allen is going through a bad period, now. Apparently, Rodgers has decided to try quicker transitions and Allen is not always sure about what to do. And he is prone to making dangerous fouls in front of the box that at least once in a game lead to real threats to LFC goal. He needs to clarify his game and his objectives to fulfil his indubitable potential.

To complete the considerations on same team sheets, in one aspect the team sheet was almost completely changed to good effect. A month ago Swansea knocked out LFC from League Cup in Anfield in an extremely poor performance by LFC. That team sheet was almost completely changed last Sunday, and with that different input it came a different output, though, as said, not in the slightest satisfactory enough. Games keep coming thick and fast, providing occasion to improve performances. Drastic improvement is really needed in LFC to try and complete what, come May, could be deemed a good season.

15.- Endless (yet interesting) debates

Date: 04/12/12
Previous matches: LFC 1-0 Southampton (Premier League); Fulham U21 1-2 LFC U21 (U21 League)

Luckily enough, football provides us with all sorts of contested issues to keep debating between fans, while at the same times provides facts for everyone to back their views.

One of such debating issues is that of players playing "out of position" or in their best position. To what extent it is advisable to play a player out of position; in what circumstances it is a good idea; when is it more beneficial than damaging to the team; they are all questions for the manager to decide and act accordingly. And also questions for the fans to keep talking about.

Football is a team game, and one can find many specific positions in which a player could eventually be deployed, depending on the different tactics and systems a manager decides to play. Sometimes there are only small adjustments so a player no doubt can easily fulfil both functions with ease.

But that is not always the case. Glen Johnson can no doubt perform as a left back, even as a left wing; but he is a right back, maybe a right wing. He has been playing at left flank for way too much time over the last months. And, being a good player, he has done OK, he has not let down the team or the managers. However, the team has been missing him on the right, as seen in last games in which he has come back there.

The tricky question to answer is whether or not the team has been better off with Kelly or Wisdom (or Henderson, or Flanagan) on the right and Johnson on the left than it would have been with Johnson on the right and Enrique or Robinson or Downing on the left. In my view, Johnson should have been kept on the right, and in that respect I feel kind of vindicated by last games; on the other hand, I cannot simply dismiss the opinion of Dalglish or Rodgers, who know better than me both, the team in particular and football in general.

Still, every one of us is entitled to our own opinion. And the game against Southampton provides plenty of food for thought in this respect. In what has probably been one of the, if not the, best game in a while for LFC, we saw Johnson as right (not left) back; Enrique as left back (not wing); Allen as playmaker, and not holding midfielder; Gerrard in a freer role; and Shelvey in an advanced position.

Along with them, Reina, Skrtel, Agger, Leiva, Sterling and Suarez all played in their favoured positions, more or less the same as the majority of games. With every player playing in their natural places on the pitch, the team looked way more comfortable than in previous matches. The football circulated better, the attacking movements were more acute, the defensive movements were more effective, and overall the level of play showed a marked improvement.

Johnson running up and down the pitch; Enrique providing the advantages of his attacking threats and runs without the setbacks of his not knowing the keys to playing up the pitch; Gerrard looking far more at ease combining the defensive and attacking sides of his game and using his knowledge to decide where and how to play in each moment; Shelvey being able to appear almost on every place of the attacking front.

And probably the more benefited for all these position changes, Allen. After a remarkably good start to the season, he was struggling in last games. The defensive duties attached to the holding midfielder in Rodgers system were taking its toll on Allen, who was losing his passing and organizing abilities while not being able to be totally efficient in his defensive tasks.

Partially liberated from the defending, he was much more involved in the game, improving the quality of possession, and the transition from defence to attack. That improved fluidity was in turn decisive to attack better, get in advancing positions with good control of the ball, and ultimately create more and better goal chances.

Obviously, not every thing was inch-perfect. The team was unable to turn their dominance into goals, and the score sheet remained threatening till the end of the match. Even if defensively the team worked well, and did not have many troubles, one can never know when a goal against can arrive. But this time the game ended with the victory. And with a point scored for those who tend to prefer to see the players playing in their natural position, even if in the process some post in the team needs to be occupied for a slightly inferior player.

With an exception, though. In the formative years the situation can be different, for educative purposes. In last games we have seen Morgan playing for the U21 as right wing. Being an outstanding goal scorer, this could be seen as a strange movement, like when, with Cruyff as manager, none other than Gary Lineker played as right wing at Barcelona. I do not know the precise rationale behind the Morgan situation, but it might be an attempt not only to use his traits for the immediate benefit of the team, but also to strengthen his qualities, adding more link abilities to his play, turning him into a more complete player.

Or maybe not, and I am reading too much into it. Anyway, the formative years are different. As well as Morgan playing as right winger, Robinson played as centre-back for the U21 against Fulham in their 2-1 away victory. Maybe to help him develop new qualities, maybe just for an emergency in that position. This U21 team is delivering many good moments this season. Hopefully things will remain similar after the promotion of Borrell to other responsibilities in the Academy.

What will most likely remain similar in the debate about players playing out of position. As happens so often in football, examples can be found to back both sides of the argument. Last games by LFC, and particularly the one against Southampton, speak for the advantages of playing the players in positions they know well. Another chapter next weekend, with the replacement of Suarez (incidentally, a striker should never have so many bookings in so few games, something that needs to be corrected) in the game against West Ham.

Let's hope the team can follow the way they have found, and keep improving. Having been a good game, the Southampton one should not be the finished article for LFC season.

16.- More growing opportunities

Date: 08/12/12
Previous matches: Udinese 0-1 LFC (Uefa Europa League); LFC U21 4-1 Crystal Palace U21 (U21 League)

Victory against Udinese on the last match of Europa League group phase saw LFC go through knock-out stages, thus providing more matches to be played in international competition. Those matches have been valuable over last seasons for LFC players who have gained experience and knowledge of different ways in which the game is played overseas. The games have been being used by different managers (Hodgson, Dalglish, and Rodgers) to prove playing alternatives in competitive matches, and offer new and young players the chance to prove themselves at demanding games.

In my view, a European competition (even if it is this kind of "second division", the Europa league) should be given fully commitment by LFC, which have made a great deal of its legend in Europe. On the other hand, it is impossible to play the better eleven in every match. So an adequate balance needs to be found. And I think that, in this 12/13 season, Rodgers has almost nailed it up to now. The starting elevens have been increasingly involving the better players and at the end some playing time has been given to fringe players and youngsters while a first spot place has been achieved at the end of group phase, in a group that has proved to be trickier than it seemed at the beginning.

It will provide the squad with at least two more matches in the competition, and hopefully many more. It is about time LFC at least makes it to the very final stages of the Europa League. It might be important in the building process in which the team is now. While the main target remains climbing up the Premier League table, cup competitions add playing opportunities, and provide types of games that are relevant to the players growing process, while protecting and enhancing the club name all over Europe.

It was not the best of games, against Udinese. But the team somewhat navigated it with ease, barring the last kick of the match, in which Di Natale almost knocked-out the team and would have entirely changed, for example, these lines. Other than that, the team barely had any difficulties in keeping a clean sheet. At the same time, the team did not really dominate the match, neither through possession nor through defending. More work is needed on that field of dominating and closing the matches, both through turning the chances into goals and through keeping the control of the match. Anyway, the match left much more positives than negatives in the end.

So, more growing opportunities for the team and players in Europe. And also growing opportunities in U21s side, which won yet another game on Friday against Crystal Palace. This team is growing at a remarkable pace, and the players in it are greatly benefiting from it. We can only hope that recent changes in staff (former team manager Borrell being made Head of Academy Coaching and Inglethorpe U21s manager) will prove to be for the better of players' development.

U21s are lately developing a trait that is both worrying and encouraging: the defence is looking a bit weak. That in itself is worrying, being a weakness in the team; on the other hand, it is a sign of a team so dominant that the defence is seldom needed; and when needed, there are certain difficulties. Hopefully, nothing than cannot be solved. Both full backs, Flanagan and Smith are of a very high level. Smith did not have the best of games against Crystal Palace, while Flanagan even scored. Both are very good prospects for the future, and look like potential first class full backs, provided they can take the final and all important steps in their growing process.

Robinson, having progressed as left back, is now learning his trade as centre-back, either as a long term project or as an emergency solution. He has conditions, although as of now he is now and then caught out of position, or making bad decisions. But overall he looked composed playing along much more experienced Sama. One of more impressive improvements this season is that of Roddan in the midfield. He used to be one of these somewhat obscure players who performed his duties, but was seldom remarkable in the possession.

This season, and in particular against Crystal Palace, he is taking a more active role, both defending and attacking. He looks increasingly comfortable on the ball, he knows where to go in each moment, and can dictate the game. He is growing fast, evolving into a much better player. Pelosi played along him, and was less brilliant, though he was helpful; but he looks a little bit confused with his frequent role and position changes.

On the attacking four, nothing really new to be said. They were terrific. And for the opposition defenders, terrifying. The attacking play by LFC U21s team is as good as it gets. The players can use the ball, can manage it, they constantly interchange their playing positions, and they can judge when it is advisable to play backwards and when and how to go forward. They are always damaging the defenders. Much of this is due to the very quality of the players. But much of it is also due to great training work, no doubt.

Moreover, that quality seems to be not dependant on particular players. On Friday, Morgan, Adorjan, Teixeira and Pacheco started; on other matches, Ngoo, Yesil can also play. And even Sinclair or Ibe, to name just a few, can figure. Not to forget that Sterling and Suso more or less also belong in this team. And apparently the level of attacking play does not diminish. They seem to be ahead of the first team on that department; obviously, it is much more difficult to play in the Premier League, so any conclusion has to be carefully taken.

But leaving aside the immediate first team future, U21s is really a team to enjoy watching, and checking the constant progress by the players involved. If in the long term it will benefit the first team, all the better; if not, at least we can have all the enjoyment of seeing the team play in these matches. Next challenge for them is their own European competition, the NextGen Series. That is an U19s competition, so the team is different, and they have struggled up to now. But they have been great in home matches and, in their last match of group stages, next January, they could still qualify for knock-out stages.

It would be great to see both, first team and U19s, still competing in Europe next year. But obviously the first team comes first, and, on that front, is mission accomplished. And it would also be great to see both teams progressing and growing to become better and better teams with better and better players.

17.- Penalties shoot-outs and lessons to learn

Date: 12/12/12
Previous matches: West Ham 2-3 LFC (Premier League)

I must confess I was still pondering what to write about last weekend LFC game against West Ham when something really extraordinary happened in the match between Bradford and Arsenal: in that match, Bradford achieved an amazing record of nine consecutive victories in penalty shoot-outs. That is truly remarkable. If we were to admit that in a penalty shoot-out the chances are 50% for each team to win, nine consecutive victories is one case in 512. I do not think many statisticians would be supporting the idea of those 50/50 chances of winning/loosing a penalty shoot-out. At least, not against the Bradford team of last three years!

Other team with a remarkable success record in penalty shoot-outs? LFC, of course. As of now, if I am not mistaken, the record is 11 wins and two defeats for LFC when matches have needed to go to penalties. Again, far away from that theoretical 50/50 chance of winning. And a team remarkably unsuccessful in penalty shoot-outs? England national team. One win and six defeats, one of the (if not the) worst record in international football. Even more so, given that the one win came immediately before being knocked out of the tournament by virtue of…penalty shoot-out (England '96). When it comes to penalty shoot-outs, luck has its role to play. But also quality of players, nerves control, accuracy, confidence, and so on. It is not just a matter of luck. That said, there is certainly much more room for luck in penalties that in regular football matches.

Regular football matches like the one between West Ham and LFC. Even though luck had also its role in the match. That was a big result for LFC, and hopefully a pivotal moment in 12/13 season. West Ham's Boleyn Ground is a very difficult place to go and get a win, and West Ham was ahead of LFC in the table before the match. So the result is great news for LFC season, now a mere four points from 4th spot. That result was both hardly fought and fortunate to an extent.

Broadly speaking, the match had three distinct spells. For about the first 20/25 minutes the match was disputed, but LFC were the better team, even if not by great margin. Johnson's spectacular goal reflected about right the developments of the match. From that 20/25 minute until Joe Cole's draw at 75th minute, West Ham were the better team. Their 2-1 partial win in those 50 minutes was probably the least West Ham deserved. Finally the last minutes were for LFC, which after finding the 3-2 comfortably navigated the rest of the match. Overall, the final result was harsh to West Ham, and generous to LFC. Not because they did not fight for it, but because West Ham fought as much without reward.

Valuable lessons can probably be learned from the match. And these are good circumstances to learn the lessons. After a defeat, one tend to try explain the defeat more than find the improvements needed; after a comfortable win, one has the risk of focusing only on the good aspects; but after a hard win one can take the positives, and appreciate them, while at the same time looking in good mood to the mistakes and the ways to better the performances.

For example, Johnson played a fantastic first half, and a good second one, mainly on the offensive, scored a great goal and caused all sorts of problems to West Ham defenders. All very true. Also true, Johnson found it extremely difficult to face Jarvis while defending. But it is probably easier to take a look at the defensive problems knowing that, after all, the match ended with a much needed win. Johnson will need to make adjustments to his defence against players like Jarvis; moreover, not only the full backs, but the entire team will need to adjust to defend against teams that make good use of the width of the pitch.

But probably the most needed adjustments are those relating to that spell of about 50 minutes in which West Ham were clearly better. It is not admissible that every long aerial football into LFC box, or even half, caused so many troubles to the defence. That needs to be corrected. And again it will be hopefully easier to correct it after a win. Probably some kind of short-term interchanging positions between Leiva and the centre-backs is needed; or maybe the full backs helping in dealing with those long balls; or more pressing up the field in order to difficult the footballs arriving. Or some kind of combination between these and other solutions. Anyway, some kinds of remedies need to be implemented to counteract that kind of tactic by opposition teams.

On the other hand, some improvements can be seen in last matches on the attacking front. Against Southampton fewer goals than deserved were scored; against West Ham, more than deserved. But in both matches the team showed more edge, more ambition, more verticality. There is still plenty of room for improvement here, but the team is showing signs of progress. Hopefully they will keep on advancing on this path and becoming a more reliable team in terms of goals scored.

That attacking improvement, that very good result, should not serve to disguise the fact that the game against West Ham were far from perfect, and that work in the training pitch is needed to be a more solid team in defence and more efficient team in front of goal. On the other hand, it would be unfair to pin exclusively on luck the victory against West Ham. Admittedly, I for one did not see Joe Cole's goal coming at the moment; but it was not just luck, but the kinds of things that happen when you have in your team first quality players like Sterling and Cole. That was a great goal, very well taken by Cole and very well created by Sterling.

And it opened the way to a much welcomed victory, which may serve as a season catalyser. A victory in which luck played some part, but in which playing ability played a big part, too. Ultimately, luck is always part and parcel of football. But if you have in your side better penalty takers, more calmed players able to hold their nerves, a goalkeeper ready for the challenge, you are likely to do a Bradford and win penalty shoot-outs time and again. If you have quality players, good passers, great shooters, players able to get in the box and quietly wait for the best moment to shoot and the best angle to put the ball in, you are likely to win more football matches.

18.- Dickensian match

Date: 19/12/12
Previous matches: LFC 1-3 Aston Villa (Premier League)

In the beginning of his infamous novel "A Tale of Two Cities", Charles Dickens wrote: "It was the best of times; it was the worst of times". To a certain extent, that was the case of last LFC match, the 1-3 defeat against Aston Villa at Anfield. The team showed during the match some of its best qualities, level of play, and capabilities; and also some of the worst football actions of the season. The best that Rodgers has achieved with the team, and the worst performances; the best football moments, the worst result.

There were good and bad things in attack and in defence; on the flanks and through the middle; at either side of the pitch. The dominant feeling after the match for LFC fans was, understandably, one of disappointment, at the very least. The match had been sort of taking for granted over the week, with the three points mentally added to LFC tally in that always elusive table climbing. That feeling might (or might not) had permeated and got to the team and players. If yes, that was arguably a first mistake; but in that case it would have been unconsciously, so there is very little anyone could have done to prevent that.

Anyway, the team entered the match with lots of energy, will, and hungry for scoring and winning. For long spells in the first half LFC looked as a storm coming at Aston Villa goal. Coming but, regrettably, not arriving. Villa defenders were repeatedly dispossessed of the football in their own half, with LFC players getting at them from seemingly everywhere. Once in possession, LFC were at their best this season, with quick and generally accurate passes, and with a good balance between keeping the ball and causing damage to the opposition.

Still, all of that came short. Short because clear cut goal chances were less than the playing deserved, mainly because last passes and crosses were not as precise as they should have been; and short because when the goal chances arrived, they were, one way or another, squandered. As a result, Villa emerged undamaged from that threatening storm. Not only that; with little collective effort, they scored not once, but twice, in the first half. Thanks mainly to great Benteke actions. The boy was on fire last Sunday, he could do no wrong on the pitch. But also thanks to weaknesses in LFC defence we have seen time and again during last seasons.

The centre of the defence gave Villa strikers every chance to get to scoring positions. And Villa strikers took those chances remarkably well; but the match showed that Leiva was possibly not ready to play so many matches after so long a spell out of the pitch, and that Skrtel was far from his best, with Reina, Allen and Agger unable to correct and prevent the goals. After the goals against, LFC certainly played with less intensity, with less belief. They were, obviously, "hard times" (title of another novel by Dickens). Still, the players showed some good intentions and an LFC goal never seemed too far away, even if it never arrive until the final moments of the match.

LFC showed some intensity, energy and edge on the attack that had been missed during this season. They finally showed a plan to turn the possession into goal chances. Possession was often put to a very good use, both controlling the game and damaging the opposition. Also the pressing high up the pitch got its rewards in the form of potentially dangerous ball steals. At the same time, the team showed weaknesses: in the final pass that was seldom precise enough to take advantage of the previous good work; in the crosses, of a worryingly poor quality almost for the entire match; in the chance conversion rate; and in the consistency. The team could not maintain the good moments of play for long enough, and lowered the intensity in various moments, to the advantage of Aston Villa.

Another weakness, as said before, was the defence. Leiva was unable to cope with a very demanding task, and his partnership with Allen did not work very well. That put Skrtel and Agger on a difficult position that they were not able to solve efficiently, particularly on this match Skrtel. So, at first sight there are two possible ways forward for LFC: trying to fix the attacking problems, or trying to fix the defending problems.

That is the kind of situation that tests the confidence and resolution of a manager and a squad. Easiest way is to fortify the defence, adding another defensive midfielder or central defender, or instructing the players not to support the attack. That may work. But that is not the LFC way. Improving the attacking side of the game, being better on the pressing high up the pitch, will in turn have good effects on the defensive balance. It is more difficult, it is more risky, it is more Liverpool. If greatness, and not mild improvement, is the goal, the team should stay its course, keep improving when on the ball, and in recovering the ball quickly. That is the hard way now, and will have more ups and downs, and disappointing moments and matches, on the way.

But it is the way to being a real football force again. Having on the pitch as many players as possible from Gerrard, Allen, Sahin, Johnson, Sterling, Shelvey, Cole, Suarez, Suso, Borini, or that permanent prospect of new attacking signing (I am not suggesting playing all of them at the same time), and improving the fluidity of the football circulating between them, increasing the tempo, the rhythm, and ball possession and game control, and extending the dominance for more time in the matches. It is not a quick process, and it would be time costing. But some glimpses of it have been showed in last matches, and there is much football in LFC players that is struggling to come to the surface.

Of course, Rodgers is the manager, and he knows much more football than I do. And the process should be balanced between attack and defence. But the emphasis should be on improving the ball possession and use. LFC fans should be given the chance to have again great expectations (yes, Dickens novel) on the team, not just the hope of some good results now and then. Returning to the beginning of "A Tale of Two Cities", this can be the "Season of Light" or the "Season of Darkness" depending not only on the results, but also on what the team shows on the pitch; not only in terms of level of play showed, but also in terms of intention, of ambition.

19.- Similar beginnings, different endings

Date: 25/12/12
Previous matches: LFC 4-0 Fulham (Premier League)

Last two league games at Anfield have seen two extremely different outcomes, from 1-3 defeat against Aston Villa to 4-0 victory against Fulham. Understandably, it has led to the feeling that the team should follow the path of Fulham match and avoid the mistakes done during the Villa one. However, it might be easier said than done.

On one hand, for the obvious reason: all teams want to win, so winning is more difficult than losing. On the other hand, because it is not so simple to determine what was it that was right in the Fulham game as opposite to the Villa game. Well, the final result is one; but to get to the final result you have to navigate the circumstances of the game. And in that front, things become trickier to analyse.

While the score stood at 0-0, both matches were pretty similar. And, if needed to chose, probably even better the Villa one. The team was sharp, pressing high, creating chances. Then, Villa goal came almost out of nowhere; in fact, two of them. And the match changed drastically. But probably the one thing that separated both games was the first goal.

Or maybe the second; still at 1-0, a long distance shot by Fulham, not very different from that of Benteke's first goal for Villa, was close to beating Reina. Should that 1-1 have gone into the score, who knows what would have happened in the rest of the match. But Reina managed to kick the ball out, and the match remained safe.

The matter can be analysed pessimistically as a weak team depending on external circumstances to deliver; or optimistically as a team still under construction that is finding its way. Pessimistically as in "Fulham could have ended as Villa did" or optimistically as in "Villa could have ended as Fulham did". Or simply as things football has.

What is true is that, as of now, a thin, thin, line is separating LFC both from winning big and from losing big. In this sense, consistency is something that the team needs to add. Both the capacity of surmounting bad circumstances and of even preventing them to occur. And in this sense a significant difference can be seen between Fulham and Villa games.

It is very good to say that "if only" Villa's goals wouldn't have happened; but the sheer truth is that Fulham almost never had the chance to score. That possibility of Fulham ruining the result by scoring was denied from the root. The defensive side of the team worked almost to perfection. Not only did not Fulham have goal chances; they seldom approached LFC box. That is more difficult that it may seem given that LFC were in front for almost the entire match, giving every incentive to Fulham to look for the equaliser.

Some of the good defending might be caused by an indifferent game by Berbatov, as opposite to Benteke; but, on LFC side, the defensive triangle of Skrtel, Agger and Leiva managed the match well. And perhaps more importantly, Shelvey was a kind of unsung hero in that respect. He added to the attack, but he really helped the midfield to deny Fulham efforts. It was one of the less brilliant, but more complete, matches Shelvey has played for LFC. It was almost like having two players on the pitch.

With the defensive platform assured, Gerrard, Downing and Suarez played good attacking movements. Suso was less involved, even though he showed his quality and potential in a couple of occasions. One particular movement seems to be rewarding for the team. The second goal, an inch-perfect pass by Downing to an inch-perfect run by Gerrard, was very similar to Joe Cole's goal after Sterling's pass against West Ham, a couple of weeks ago. More than likely, something that it is being worked on during the trainings in Melwood.

Not only we have seen two similar goals in a short period of time; in fact, a similar run by Suarez ended with him on the ball inside Fulham box that in the end did not become a goal, but came close (after all, one cannot win every time). Those kinds of running and passing movements might be instrumental to providing the team with the needed edge on the attack, one way to turning possession into goal chances and eventually goals. It cannot be the one and only weapon, but it can be a powerful one.

All the good news, however, should not disguise the fact that the team was far from perfect, even if winning 4-0. There were not so many clear goal chances, and very often the team defended in its own half, without really pressing Fulham players. While that might be the appropriate thing to do in that particular match under those particular circumstances, if the aim of the team is to become a real dominant force, it will be necessary to keep building the defensive and attacking sides of the team.

Fulham game may point to a path to follow, but that path needs to be followed, not considered as the finished article. At least, the team is progressing, and progressing after a clear win is easier; but the analysis should go deeper than the results. Villa's game was not only bad, and contained aspects that worked well and should be kept in the team; Fulham's game was not only good, and contains aspects that should be drastically improved.

Games come thick and fast in the festive period, and one week from now three more league games will have been played. Games with both, the label of "winnable" and the label of "dangerous", clearly visible in them. Hopefully the endings will be more like the Fulham game, whereas it would not be a bad thing if the beginnings looked similar to the Villa's game. With the team still a work in progress, it would be wise not to dismiss some good traits hided in bad final outcomes. Against Villa, LFC showed good beginnings and remarkable resilience even if the final result was negative; against Fulham, some defensive errors were corrected and the improved conversion rate of goal chances resulted in a much better final score.

20.- Getting ready for prime time

Date: 27/12/12
Previous matches: Stoke 3-1 LFC (Premier League)

Classic TV show Saturday Night Live (SNL) started in 1975, and is still alive and kicking. One of the most successful TV shows ever, and deservedly so. The show includes a guest star, and a regular cast, performing live comedy sketches. In its first sessions, the regular cast of the show, including stars as bright as John Belushi, Dan Aykroyd, Joan Curtin, Chevy Chase, Gilda Radner, Laraine Newman, Garret Morris, or, shortly after, Bill Murray, used to be known as the "Not Ready for Prime Time Players".

Clearly that nick name was just one of the jokes: they all were more than ready for prime time. Still, the original term includes two different assertions; on the negative side, that they were supposedly not ready for performing at first class stage. On the positive side, the assumption that maybe they could be ready in the near future, as in the "not (yet) ready", given the appropriate time and chances.

Those reflections came to me while watching the 3-1 defeat by LFC at Stoke. I am afraid that, as of now, LFC squad contains too many not (yet?) ready for prime time players. They all have in them quality; one player does not make it to LFC first squad without some special talent. But many of them are not ready no perform consistently at Premier League, in front of experienced and also talented players. They can offer glimpses of their talent now and then, they can be inspired in a given match; but they are not able no keep their level up to LFC standards.

Hence, the team goes from a solid 4-0 win against Fulham to a deserved 3-1 defeat at Stoke in a 4-day period. It not being the first time something similar has happened, turning this season in a roller-coaster of hope and despair, in which pundits can set the maximum expectations for LFC on a first-half-of-the-table finish, and a top four, or even top three, within few days. And, in a sense, they all have a point. At their best, one can imagine LFC players climbing up the table with almost no limit. When far from their best, it is difficult to think they could go over the 10th place. At this point in time, the team as a whole is not ready for prime time.

That level of uncertainty, of lack of consistency, is typical of being not ready for performing at first level. Stoke players will never show the brilliancy LFC players are capable of in their good days; equally true, you will never find sharp ups and downs in Stoke performance; they are a reliable team, with few oscillations, both for the best and for the worst. They are probably not ready for prime time in the sense of winning titles, but they are well in control of their expectations and capacities.

It is good to have some players not yet ready in the team. Getting ready is a steady process, except in the case of real stars. And introducing little by little new players is the way for them to become ready. The problem arises when the not ready players are almost the majority of the team. In that case, the likely outcome is that the grown players underperform. That delicate balance is now where LFC seems to be. When at least some of the up and coming players manage to perform to the level of the first class payers, they can drag with them the rest of the players and the team excels, or at least plays well.

When few or none of the not ready players manages to play to LFC standards, even the senior players find it impossible to deliver, and the team offers a lacklustre performance. As of now, LFC squad has no more than four/five regular ready for prime time players (Reina, Johnson, Gerrard, Suarez, maybe Agger), and many not (hopefully yet) ready (Suso, Sterling, Allen, Shelvey, Sahin, Henderson, Borini, maybe Leiva). While the squad is unbalance in that respect, there can be hope that some of these players become ready in the near future. After all, even such accomplished stars as John Belushi and Dan Aykroyd grew even while with SNL and became not only ready for prime time players, but in fact real stars, in TV, music, and films, as the Blues Brothers.

More complicated is the case of not so young players as Downing, Enrique, or Skrtel. They are not ready, and unlikely to be ready in the future. They are competent players, even Premier league players, but not LFC players, if that means aiming at the top of the table. While the three of them have scored this season, and have occasionally shone, they have inconsistencies in their play. Not for the first time, in the games against West Ham, Aston Villa, and Stoke, Skrtel has been unable to cope with aerial challenges from opposition with due authority. Enrique and Downing are capable of taking the pitch by storm in their good moments, but spend long spells almost unseen. They can accompany the team, they can raise their own level with other players, but they cannot raise the level of the other players, they cannot consistently impact matches by themselves.

Out of this scheme, Carragher and Cole are different cases; both were undoubtedly ready for prime time players time ago. Both can help the team, and both have helped, both are possibly worth having in the squad. But they are not the ones to sustain the team. They can add to the team, and maybe be of much help in turning the youngsters into first team players. The problem with this squad is that it is a difficult environment for young players to get ready while at the same time delivering results. Not impossible, but a real challenge for manager and staff. The risk is overburdening the not ready players to an extent that instead of impelling their growing, it ends up ending it.

While games come fast, nurturing process should be made compatible with first class performances and getting results. There is not a proven formula to conclude the process, and LFC can only hope that Rodgers and their staff are capable of building a ready for prime time team. For that to happen, the current not ready for prime time players will need to step up. At least, they can look for encouragement to that first "Not Ready for Primer Time Players" that became real legends in show business, setting the foundations for a TV show that keeps offering laughter and entertainment so many years after its beginnings.

21.- New Year balances and wishes

Date: 01/01/13
Previous matches: QPR 0-3 LFC (Premier League)

Every January comes with its share of balances and prospects for the New Year. Despite everyone being well aware that there is no much difference between this day and any other, it is a good moment for revising the year gone. LFC wise, 2012 has not been a particularly good year. It started with Dalglish at the helm, and a promising run in the league (34 points in 19 games) while the team was in League Cup semi-finals. Not a bad starting point, short of what LFC fans expect from the team, but not the worst scenario. However, a much worse second half of league season (18 points in 19 games) seemed to be a huge step back. On the other hand, more silverware came to Anfield in the form of the League Cup, and Wembley became sort of a familiar space for LFC, which almost achieved a remarkable double, had it not been for a narrow defeat in FA Cup final.

In the end, league form in the second half of the season took its toll, and it was decided that Dalglish would leave the post as manager. Probably equally as important was that, generally speaking, his signings, some of them very expensive, failed to really deliver, and the fact that, league wise, the team looked like going down, not up. All in all, LFC opted for a new project under a young manager who had excelled with Swansea, both in terms of results and in terms of the type of play seen played by a so-called "lesser" team.

Up until now, the objective balance, 28 points in 20 league games (meaning that, on a calendar year, LFC's tally is 46 points in 39 games; that is relegation form), knocked out at Anfield in League Cup, and qualified for knock-out stages in Europa League as first of the group, is similar to Hodgson's, and worse than Dalglish's. Even in the fact that many young and fringe players have been used in European competition. Well, Hodgson reached 25 points in his 20 first league games, and was evicted from the League Cup in a much more embarrassing game, against Northampton. But the overall picture is similar in numbers.

Even so, general feeling at Anfield seems to be much more positive than under Hodgson. The team have offered some glimpses of good football, and some convincing matches, along with the disappointments and lack of consistency that have regrettably become usual at LFC during last seasons. The squad is much younger now, and there is hope it can keep improving and reaching new heights in the more or less near future. And, overall, there is some perception that Rodgers has a plan and he is making some kind of progress.

What was probably decisive in Hodgson dismissal was the feeling that he was just navigating the present, not being able to convey the idea that he was laying foundations for a better future. Rodgers has been much better at that. Questions now are whether he really has a plan, and whether that plan will be successful. January transfer window might provide a hint on the path Rodgers is looking for, both in terms of type(s) of player(s) signed and in terms of the ambition in the profile of those players.

But the real test will the 18 remaining league games, more so even than the runs in cups. The team will need to achieve something in the region of 35 points in those matches to be convincing of going forward. Whatever the circumstances, bad luck, injuries, woodwork, squandered chances, refereeing, and the like, around 35 points, with a total league tally of 60 plus might leave a good sensation. Obviously, being able to approach the 40 points from now for a total of near 70 would stand the team in very good stead going into next season. But that is probably unrealistic, as of now.

That is not to say that league results are the only thing. They could be qualified by cup runs, quality of play displayed, performances by the team, signs of improvement, and so on, especially the general feeling (or lacking of) that the team is evolving, is improving, is building to be better. But numbers do matter, too, to fans and to owners, to current players and to staff, to journalists and to prospective players. LFC need to be seen as consolidated as a real force in world football by offering a credible chance to first enter in Champions League again and then challenge for titles.

In the short term, January offers an uphill way in League, with visits to Old Trafford and the Emirates. So, 2013 comes with demanding beginnings that might set the tone, for the worse or for the better. We don't know yet if there will be reinforcements for those matches, and who they might be. For a New Year wish, I would really like a world class central defender. While I can see that the squad needs a striker to either support or cover Suarez, a sustained good run without improving the defending seems impossible; at least one central defender is been needed for years. Anyway, defender or striker (or both), what is really needed for new additions is that they are really an improvement over what LFC already have at Anfield (or Melwood, or Kirkby) now.

Current squad has been able to complete some really good matches. And they have finished 2012 is style, with a 3-0 away win at QPR. It was a very good first half, in which QPR were not given a single chance to even fight the match. It was as if LFC players were able to pass on, in football terms, the bug that rallied the LFC expedition before the game. That first half was as hard a football demolition as they come. Fans always want more, so more ambition in the second half, really tearing apart the opposition with a goal festival, would have been a good New Year gift for the fans. But I would gladly welcome any 3-0 win over the rest of the season. Not only the win, but also that sense of the opposition not having the slightest chance; that is important, too, and the team excelled in that.

So may that end to 2012 be a good indication of what is coming in 2013. A growing team that ends the season on a real high, that progresses in their way to become a real football force again on the pitch.

22.- Winning by the book

Date: 03/01/13
Previous matches: LFC 3-0 Sunderland (Premier League)

Football is sometimes praised for being unpredictable and open to surprises. Some matches end up with results difficult to have been predicted before the match. Other times, the final outcome is surprising given the development of the game, with the better team being defeated. LFC have found themselves on the bad side of both types of unexpected outcomes. To be fair, LFC have also been on the good side of those types of matches at certain times. Inevitably, almost every fan remembers much more the "injustices" against than the "injustices" in favour. Overall, those types of matches add both frustration and joy to football, and are one reason for football to be praised by pundits and be so broadly followed.

However, football is often predictable, with matches unfolding more or less as expected, and with final results being fair reflects of what happened on the pitch. More than that, there are some matches that have an almost "perfect" structure of actions that carry the match softly, steadily, to its, more than expected, inevitable final outcome. One such match was LFC vs. Sunderland at Anfield.

The game started disturbingly for LFC in its first minutes. Sunderland were there to fight, and fight hard, for the victory. Sunderland players were pressing up the field, making it difficult for LFC to get the football out of defence in a controlled way. At the same time, they were aggressive, pushing to be around LFC box and trying to create goal chances. So the first task for LFC was to overcome that challenge, to find a way to deactivate that pressure, those difficulties.

That first task was accomplished by way of Gerrard and Henderson helping the team where needed, and by the great contribution by Reina to the distribution of the football. So, slowly but steadily, LFC gained control of the game, and could start to get forward. Secondly, once the team had some control of the football and the game, the team needed to find ways in which the opposition could be damaged. So, LFC players started to raise the pressure on Sunderland players and to exchange passes in dangerous zones.

Thirdly, and perhaps more importantly, an opening goal was going to be an almost decisive stroke. And it came. To be fair, LFC was only starting to deserve that goal, with few clear chances before. But a combination of good player placement, good aerial challenge won by Gerrard, and an incredibly smart and accurate pass by Suarez ended up with Sterling scoring. That first goal topped the first phase of the match. LFC had prevailed after a difficult start and was in front.

But it would not have been the first time in which a similar situation was squandered by LFC. Not this time; the demolition work continued. After a few moments in which Sunderland threatened with an equaliser and some adjustments were necessary, and in which Reina had a relevant part to play in a couple of occasions, LFC were ruthless in stopping Sunderland and attacking them time and again. Remarkably, and contrary to what had happened at times, second half came with the same attitude, the same quest for goal, the same dominance on the pitch.

Sunderland had not the slightest hope of a recovery, with LFC defensive mechanisms working to perfection, and how the match ended with only three goals for LFC appeared a mystery at the end. Part of it was, of course, due to a lack of concentration of the players in that they were caught off-side twice; part of it, bad luck, bad finishing, good goalkeeping. All in all, a perfect scheme; first, taking control of the game; then, taking advantage on the score sheet; then, showing authority and ambition to finish the game while conceding no chances to opposition. Winning by the book.

In general, the better match as a whole played by LFC for a while. Glimpses of brilliance have been there to be seen in other matches, but this has been the best overall display in much time. Each and every player performed more than well, and probably almost anyone deserves to be recognised. But I would like to single out the importance of three of them. Firstly, Suarez was omnipresent, always dangerous, always inflicting damage to the opposition, tirelessly working. His assist in the first goal and finishing in second and third were inch-perfect. Secondly, Gerrard was a joy to watch; he commanded the game from midfield, moving the football around, choosing when to play long, when to play short, when to control, when to be aggressive. A player at his peak of knowledge of the game;

and his pass in the third goal, absolutely superb. Thirdly, Downing was extremely good in supporting the attack from the flank. He run, dribbled, crossed; but he also came inside when needed. His movement in the third goal provided the space Suarez needed to run and Gerrard needed to pass. Great game by him, with an understanding with Johnson that was growing with the game.

As said before, the rest of players played also very well, and the team as a whole was at great level. Obviously, not to forget that the game was not by any means perfect. It would be a bad sign if the team thought that this is the finished article, and they have achieved the target as to how to play. And surely the staff will not allow that to happen. There were some individual mistakes that can be corrected, and some bad decisions; there were little gaps in focus that in other circumstances could have been costly. There were some misunderstandings between players. Obviously, one could never avoid every mistake, but one can work to reduce them.

Most importantly, the players have two challenges in front of them. On one hand, reproduce this kind of performance in front of top teams. With ManU, Arsenal, and Man City games coming soon, the team will need to prove that they are up to the challenge. On the other hand, show this kind of performance on a most consistent basis. Mansfield and Norwich will provide the next opportunities in this front.

For the moment, 3-0 victories either side of New Year Eve have been a great way to finish and begin a year. A good finishing and beginning by the book.

23.- All's well that ends well?

Date: 08/01/13
Previous matches: Mansfield 1-2 LFC (FA Cup)

In his play "All's Well That Ends Well", Shakespeare seems at first sight to clearly state that if something ends well, then everything is OK. But, on second thoughts, it is not so clear, even in the very Shakespeare's play, which is now broadly considered as a "problem" play, more than a "comedy". All kinds of nuances arise from the presumed "well" status in the end. After past weekend FA Cup match at Mansfield, LFC have been left at a similar "problem" regarding the outcome of the match. On one hand, there is the performance by the team, far from good enough, even if the win was achieved; on the other hand, the controversy following the handball by Suarez in his goal, even if the goal stood.

This year, LFC were one potential victim of the tricky third round of the FA Cup, playing away at Mansfield, a Conference team. As it turned out, the big disappointment for LFC was avoided in that LFC managed to win the match and is now safely in fourth round. So, in that sense, a good day at the office, and eyes on ManU next Sunday. However, there is always more in football that only the result. Even more so, perhaps, if a team is under construction, if a new project is developing, as it is the case with Rodgers' LFC. In that respect the outcome is not so satisfactory.

Regarding the handball, my take is that Suarez handed the ball instinctively though deliberately (meaning he moved his arm towards the football, but he had not the time to really consider it), and the goal should have not stood. And it would have not, had the referee seen the action (I think). Obviously I might be wrong, but that is what I saw. Now, there is all the noise around that, with some accusing Suarez of cheating and some stating that one should aim for every advantage possible in professional sport.

Probably the sensible voice is that of opposition manager Paul Cox, admitting that he would have had no complaints had a similar decision come his way. Suarez did not more, not less, that almost (if not every) footballer does day in day out: try to score while avoiding the opposition to score. Many usual football actions may be considered as cheating, from diving in opposite box looking for a penalty to diving in own box looking for a foul that ends the attack; from pulling shirts when the ball is not around to pretending not to have fouled a rival; and so on. In every case, decision is left to referees. What Suarez did is no different from what many players do in every football match; at least, he did not openly celebrate his goal.

So that might just be seen as simply a refereeing mistake that this time has gone for, not against, LFC. I see that point, and accept its rationale. But that does not prevent me from wishing that Suarez had not handed the ball, or had admitted his handballing. Not that there is anything particularly wrong with what Suarez did, but it would have been a nice gesture, nothing else. I am not claiming any higher moral standard; I would probably be perfectly OK if something similar happens against ManU and the goal counts. But I don't think LFC should need those types of goals to win against a Conference team, and I reckon that in such matches one could self-impose certain rules in this respect. But, as it went, all ended well for Suarez and LFC in that goal, so in a sense all was well.

While there can be certain controversy regarding the handball, it is more worrying the way LFC played, especially in the second half. In that sense, I don't think that all was well just because it ended well. LFC started the game playing well, focused on the match, and trying to make the differences in quality between the teams and players count. That was the correct attitude, and players and staff did well in their preparation for the match. And it paid rewards in little time; best rewards possible from LFC point of view, with a goal by Sturridge.

And a great goal, it was. Allen found Shelvey unmarked in midfield, Sturridge run through the space, and Shelvey took exactly the time needed for his defence-splitting pass to find its way to Sturridge, who put the ball away with ease. Great goal, really, and the match exactly where Rodgers would have wanted it. From that moment on, LFC kept its absolute dominance of the game in the first half, and were close to scoring again. But little by little players were losing their focus, their urge for a second goal. Match seemed so under control that the players forgot to effectively control it.

Nothing wrong happened during first half, and, overall, LFC were way above Mansfield, only lacking that second goal. A quiet second half seemed on sight, but it was not to be. Just after half-time, it looked as if LFC thought that the match had ended, 45 minutes too early. LFC displayed an extremely poorly performance in second half, something that should worry the club and the fans. Mansfield absolutely outplayed LFC for long spells, and the not disallowing of Suarez goal was not the only moment in which LFC counted on Lady Luck to finally win the match.

During the second half, the team failed to properly defend against a lesser team. And failed with and without the ball. Every aerial long ball was an unsolvable problem for LFC defenders, who were unable to keep Mansfield outside LFC box; every second ball was a threat. That is something that has already been seen in Premier League matches, and needs to be corrected. It is far too easy for opposition teams to put LFC in danger when the team shows some weakness. Answer might be to defend up, to put a third central defender on the team, to play a more physical holding midfielder, to increase the pressure on the opposition players to prevent them from throwing long balls, and so on. I am certain Rodgers knows much better than me. But something needs to be done on that side.

Things were not better when on the ball. LFC could hardly keep hold of the ball during second half, which would have helped to control the game. Possession has been one of the mantras by Rodgers, and in some games it has been very good. Even in the first half against Mansfield it was not perfect, but not bad. But in the second half LFC midfielders were absolutely outplayed by the opposition. Partly lack of focus; partly a bad pitch; partly the defenders staying too near the box; partly bad playing;

partly poor decisions. The fact was that the ball spent hardly any time in LFC feet.

A very poor second half. With some good points, though, apart from the final result. Suarez showed his usual sharpness and commitment, making the most of the few chances he had. Downing kept growing; he seems to be finally finding his place in the team, and played well, being of great help to the team; Carragher performed some of his heroics in defending.

But overall a very poor second half. It certainly ended well with LFC through the fourth round. However, not even Shakespeare would have think that "all is well" with respect to the match. Hopefully the players and staff will take the chance to having seen the mistakes to try correcting them and keep progressing and improving their football, in what are going to be an extremely challenging weeks ahead.

24.- Still not there

Date: 15/01/13
Previous matches: ManU 2-1 LFC (Premier League)

LFC were in a good spell of play and results prior to the game against ManU, and some expectation was in place to check to what extent that kind of form could be seen in a match as big as they come: away, against the team at the top of the table that happened to be exactly the main rival. So it was a big match; not just in terms of league table, but in terms of checking the real progress made by the team, and the size of the task ahead.

There are a few possible, mixed, interpretations of what happened on the pitch. It is not the first time something similar happens during last seasons, in which LFC seems to be under a constant, and never finished, process of construction. Broadly speaking, a poor first half was followed by an encouraging second half; a disappointing result was accompanied by some improving signs; a weak attitude in the beginning of the match turned into a much more positive approach at the end.

The match started with LFC behaving as a lesser team, showing too much respect for their rivals. ManU played well, that is true, but they did not find many difficulties from LFC players, who seemed to be convinced of their own inferiority. In that first half, match was decided on the midfield. Carrick and Cleverley outplayed Lucas and Allen, who were nowhere near their opponents, neither on the ball nor on defence. LFC attackers did not get even the chance to take part in the game, while LFC defenders coped about right with what was thrown at them.

Thanks to that defensive performance the game was still 1-0 at half time, but the superiority by ManU was almost absolute. Action, decisive action, was needed at half-time. And decisive action was indeed taken. I do not think many LFC fans saw the kind of action that Rodgers decided coming, with Sturridge on for Leiva. Given that midfield weakness had been key to first half developments, it was a bold movement at least. But a movement that proved to be exactly what the team needed at the moment.

Second half was a completely different story. LFC came into the pitch with different attitude, and resolute to take the match to ManU. New midfield configuration, mainly with a new role for Gerrard, worked much better. "The best defence is a good attack", is often said; and in this case it was. Not that it is something automatic, of course; but sometimes reinforcing the attack is useful, and this match was one of those cases.

One of the lessons of the first half is that Leiva is not ready for highly challenging matches. More than something physical (Carrick and Cleverley are not exactly the most physical pair in the Premier League), it is likely related to that elusive idea of the "rhythm" of matches, of being fully fit to read the matches and act accordingly, after many time on the sidelines. However, the main change was the mentality of the whole team. The players entered the pitch on the second half with a completely different attitude.

Managers send messages to their players in various ways. One of those ways is the substitutions. Once it was decided that Leiva was to be substituted, given that, for whatever reason, he was not up to the game, his replacement was not a foregone conclusion. Rodgers could have opted to replace him with, say, Coates, and argued that he wanted to cement the midfield and liberate the full-backs, and encourage his players to go in the offensive; but, as likely as not, that substitution would have sent the wrong message: that the team needed mainly to improve the defence. With the introduction of Sturridge, Rodgers took a risk, a really big risk, which might have resulted in the team being totally outplayed in midfield, even more than in the first half.

However, he rightly judged what the players needed, and sent the right message: LFC needed to go after ManU and improve its defending by way of improving the attack. That was the right thing to do, and was fruitful in terms of play, if not result. LFC were better than ManU in the second half; it was not enough to avoid the defeat, and probably it was overall a fair result, given that the difference between the teams was bigger in the first half. But LFC played on ManU half, barely had to defend, and had several goal chances.

Sturridge indeed played his part, but it was not only him. Repeatedly in the second half LFC players appeared in ManU half in huge numbers. While in first half Suarez was isolated in his fight against defenders, in second half he had not only Sturridge, but 4, 5, 6, LFC players to play with. Reversely, ManU had much more problems in developing its game.

Finally, it was not to be, and the match ended in defeat. But there were valuable lessons to learn. For some weeks now, Rodgers has been time and again talking about consistency as key target for the team. Nothing to object, that is a very important target; but this match was more about another key concept, confidence. Some comfort might be found in that second half performance. But it is one thing to throw everything at the rivals once you have nothing to lose because you are already losing; and a very different thing to have the self-confidence to go for the match from the beginning. Full credit to Rodgers for his changing of the match. But the first half performance is a reminder, if needed, that the team is not quite there, that it is still work in progress. Following weeks will provide more details of the progress made and progress remaining.

All in all, reasons for pessimism and reasons for optimism. All in all, the team seems to be not very far away, but still not there where it belongs. All in all, eyes turned to Emirates and City of Manchester where similar challenges wait for the team in coming weeks.

25.- Wish you were here

Date: 24/01/13
Previous matches: LFC 5-0 Norwich (Premier League)

Music legends Pink Floyd released in 1975 one of their (many) great records, Wish You Were Here. During the 5-0 demolition of Norwich past Saturday one could not help but think that probably LFC wish Norwich were always "here", in front of them on a football pitch. Last matches between LFC and Norwich have been nothing short of a huge relief for LFC, whether LFC form was better or worse before the game.

And even whether LFC actually played better or worse during the match. Irrespective of that, LFC goals keep coming against Norwich. In this last match, however, LFC did play well, very well at times, and the final result was nothing more than deserved. It was not a perfect match, but it was close to it. Almost every player gave a good, or very good, account of themselves.

One sign of how well things went for LFC was the clean sheet. It was not absolutely indispensable given the five goals for LFC, but a clean sheet is always important for players, a nice feeling for supporters, and a good sign of progress and solidity of the team. Moreover, it is testimony to the dominance of LFC that in fact Norwich seldom threatened Jones. Some half-chances, but a Norwich goal was never on sight.

So the defensive system worked well, no doubt; even so, it would be difficult to say that Carragher, Agger, and Leiva played particularly well. They did their job, and more than rightly answered every question thrown at them, but they did not need to shine, which speaks of how well the team as a whole managed the match against a Norwich side which is far from being a weak team.

Building from that control of the game, players were on the attack time and again. In almost every moment LFC looked to have more players than Norwich on the pitch, being able to create superiorities on every part of Anfield. And clearly LFC players enjoyed the game; and as likely as not they were left wishing Norwich were here more often.

That was not the only "wish you were here" that could be seen around. Both Suarez and Sturridge seem to be wishing to play together. Second goal against Norwich was a masterpiece of simplicity and efficiency, and team are enormously benefitting from the introduction of Sturridge. Not that he is playing as a classic lone striker; he is constantly up and down the pitch, running right and left. But with Sturridge LFC have much more presence in opposition half and much more possibilities to play good football and create goal chances.

The arrival of Sturridge has reinforced one improving trend already in place a month ago, that of Downing's. He is playing better and better, and appears to be nearing the form that turned him into a promising international player some years ago. He is still inconsistent at times, and needs to keep improving, but is of great help to the team in these last matches. If he can keep his form, he can finally become the player Dalglish signed and LFC supporters have been wishing to be "here" (at Anfield) for several months by now.

Left flank was left for Johnson against Norwich, and he excelled in that role. He is no doubt a right back, and is better on the right. But he can do a job on the left, and in this match he did a magnificent job, being completely unplayable for Norwich players. He was a constant threat, very often combining with Suarez on the left flank. On this form, he is a player extremely difficult to defend, and helps greatly to the attack. That was the player we saw against Norwich.

In midfield, Henderson is quietly but steadily cementing his place in the starting eleven. In games like these, he can always find where and when to go, helping the defence when necessary and supporting the attack when appropriate; and last Saturday even opening the score. Every player played well and did their part. But the man who looked almost as flying was Gerrard. In the beginning of the season, he struggled to find his role on the pitch, sometimes caught out of position.

But over the last games, he is enjoying his football, and making the team play around him. He is almost inventing a new football role; not a holding midfielder, not an attacking midfielder, not playing on the hole behind the striker, not on either flank. Not on any of those positions, but somewhat in every one of them. He moves to the place and take the action that might be most beneficial for the team, defending, passing, attacking. Short passing, long passing, carrying the football. Looking for the decisive pass, shooting from distance, crossing the ball.

It is true that Norwich players never got anywhere near to him, and that Gerrard has had difficulties in other games; but in this particular match he masterminded the role of the complete midfielder. Definitely, wish he was here for long time.

But Norwich will not be here for the remaining of the season. LFC have improved in dealing with so called lesser teams, but have had problems with top teams. And for the team to climb the table results will need to come against top teams, too. Next two League matches, away against Arsenal and Man City, will help to assess where are LFC in terms of competing with the better teams, what are the chances of keeping the good form and finishing the league in close to the top places.

First, though, is Oldham in FA Cup. And, while the fans can keep an eye on those Premier games, the players will need to focus on Oldham and keep the momentum going. I am sure every one at LFC wishes FA Cup is "here", at Anfield, come the end of the season.

26.- Hitting the woodwork

Date: 29/01/13
Previous matches: Oldham 3-2 LFC (FA Cup)

When Gerrard hit the woodwork in the 90th minute of the FA Cup game against Oldham, it sounded just as if LFC were, yet again, on a familiar ground. For years now, the club has been struggling to come back to where it belongs, to where it used to be in its golden years. But, for one thing or another, the target is never fully achieved. The final step is always elusive, and it seems that LFC, as a club, is repeatedly hitting the woodwork, almost getting there but never arriving.

The whole game looked as a metaphor, with a combination of big mistakes, bad luck, hope, and final disappointment. And, to round it up, a final woodwork. In last seasons, woodwork has been a known enemy to LFC on the pitch (at the very least, as seen by the fans), preventing some goals to count. Against Oldham, it happened again. Had that Gerrard's shoot gone in, LFC would be facing a replay, and FA Cup hope would still be alive. However, the woodwork stood in the way, and now the club has its second Cup disappointing of the season, after the League Cup.

Anyway, it would be blatantly unfair to blame the woodwork. They were, no doubt, the very mistakes by LFC which are primarily to blame for the exit of the FA Cup against a League One opposition. Admittedly it is easier to speak with hindsight, but the selection of the starting eleven did not look right. Should the team had won, we would be speaking about the need to have rested the best attacking players; having lost, as it is the case, the best defending players were missed. At the end of the day, the attack only managed to score twice, while the defence conceded nothing less than three goals. Neither of them did a good job.

But it is the defence which, in the first half, seemed weaker. Changes at defence are particularly risky in that it is possible that the players play individually well and still the defence at a whole is dysfunctional for lack of understanding. To an extent, that could be seen against Oldham, especially on the left flank with Coates and Robinson seeming almost like perfect strangers to one another. On the right side, Wisdom and Skrtel are more used to playing together, but they were not at their best, really, allowing some dangerous crosses and attacking actions by Oldham. On the centre, Skrtel and Coates do not play well together, as shown time and again. This time, however, Skrtel hold his post, and it was Coates who had a very bad game, unable to cope with the challenge posed by Oldham strikers. Most probably, Coates needs to be playing games in order to be the promising youngster he once was and fulfil the expectations created by his signing. But, as of now, he is not ready to play at LFC if he is going to play the way he did on Sunday. At left back, I found Robinson played OK; he had his mistakes and difficulties, but more or less he did his job, even if he could have done more in the third goal.

But to focus solely on defence (as I have just done) would be unfair. Defending is a team job. And the second mistake by Rodgers, besides choosing the starting eleven, was to play without enough midfielders. Allen and Henderson were totally outplayed by opposition. Defending, they could not prevent the football arriving near Jones' box; attacking, they could not keep hold of the football, dictate the rhythm, and put order on the game; Sterling and Borini were not able to fill the midfield, and as a result LFC lost the control of the game, and the strikers seldom found the ball during the first half.

Notwithstanding that, there is no denying LFC were unfortunate to be 1-3 down shortly after the halftime; one goal conceded in the nick of halftime after a mistake by Jones; one goal squandered by Borini few seconds into the second half; and another goal conceded immediately. Little later, Gerrard and Downing substituted Wisdom and Borini, and the second half looked different. Partly because Oldham were already two goals up; partly because LFC stepped up its game.

For about twenty minutes, LFC played in fact very well, and it was just a coincidence they did not score. Defence had fewer problems, Henderson as a right back supported the attack much often than Wisdom had done, Downing caused all sorts of problems, and Gerrard organised everything. Sturridge found more space and chances, and had a couple of good goal chances. But, the goal not coming, the nerves started to take the best of the players, and precision was lost. Even so, after Allen goal, there were a couple of good chances to get the equaliser, and that woodwork by Gerrard could have saved the day for LFC.

But LFC stumbled, once again, against the woodwork. As they have been doing of late, as a team and as a club, they fought to make amends for some initial mistakes, and got good achievements in the process to rebuild, but, either because of internal mistakes, or because of external circumstances, they seem to always find woodwork in their way, very often in the final steps. They did again against Oldham, and there will be no Wembley trips this season. Still, plenty to fight for, both in Europa League and in the Premier League, starting immediately against Arsenal and Man City. The current squad is a work in progress, and next matches can give an idea of the state of that process. The team was in good form prior to this last match, and hopefully they can regroup and give a good account of themselves in coming matches. And hopefully woodwork will stand away of their way.

27.- "Yes, but no"

Date: 01/02/13
Previous matches: Arsenal 2-2 LFC (Premier League)

My three-year-old nephew has kind of developed an idiom I like very much, it is very expressive. He often says this "yes, but no". Period. No additional explanation, no further considerations; simply, "yes, but no". Usually, he uses it when speaking about look-alikes, as in "Listen, this big rock looks like a hippopotamus, doesn't it?" (Hippopotamus being one of my nephew's favourite animals); "Yes, but no". Meaning that yes, it looks like a hippopotamus, but no, it is not a hippopotamus. Hence, "yes, but no".

I was reminded of this expression when first watching and then thinking about LFC match against Arsenal, and its consequences in LFC season. On one hand, yes, LFC is able to go to Emirates and get to a 2-0 lead well into the second half; on the other hand, no, LFC cannot complete the win in the match. Yes, but no.

Yes, LFC players can complete a whole first half of competing against Arsenal and, even with the logical difficulties, ran out winners of the half. No, LFC cannot maintain the level in the second half to consolidate the victory. Yes, but no.

Furthermore, it is kind of "déjà-vu" for LFC, who often offer signs of improvement and of being nearing the level of the top teams, only to little later get back to bad performances and results. During last seasons, LFC either have been consistent against top teams but suffer against lesser teams or the complete opposite, showing consistency against lesser teams but losing against top teams, as it is the case in this 12/13 season. Either have excelled in cup games and failed in league games or been knocked-out at first stages in cup competitions and done more or less well in the league. Yes, but no.

In 12/13, after understandably struggling in first matches, LFC looked as reaching good level since mid December, and started to climb the table with a good string of results. Then the match against ManU looked to come in good time for LFC, and seemed to be a good occasion to test the real level of the team. Yet again, "yes, but no". After a poor first half, and being 2-0 down shortly after half-time, LFC gave a very convincing performance for a long period in the second half, falling just little short of at least dragging a draw from the game. Reasons for optimism and reasons for pessimism in the same game. Yes, but no.

Approaching the game at Emirates, the situation seemed similar to the moments before the game at Old Trafford, the team facing a test of being able to stand up at big stages against top teams, even mounting a credible challenge for a top four finish. During the first half the team coped well with a demanding opponent. With the help of Lady Luck in Suarez's goal and of the great performance by Reina at the other end of the pitch, a good match. Not particularly brilliant, but good.

Johnson caused problems to Arsenal defence, Henderson kept improving his game, Sturridge looked dangerous and in good understanding with Suarez, Carragher and Agger solid; over all, Gerrrard looked omnipresent, always in the right place at the right moment. Even if Arsenal can also claim to have deserved something more of the game, at half-time things were going fairly well for LFC. But in the second half the players were unable to sustain the demands of the game.

Arsenal pressed higher up the pitch, and LFC midfield was unable to keep the football and dictate the rhythm, even during short spells. Even so, LFC managed to score its second goal, in a combination of god luck and brilliance from Henderson, alone against the whole Arsenal defence. But Arsenal kept recovering the ball time and again, and closer and closer to LFC box. Inevitably, goals came and the match was drawn with more than 20 minutes to play. At that moment, things were looking very threatening for LFC.

But with the introduction of Enrique, the tiredness taking its toll from Arsenal, and certain improvement by LFC, truth is that there were less goal chances for Arsenal than could have been expected. And Suarez could even have won the game in the nick of time. Anyway, a draw is a fair result for LFC, taking into account the game as a whole. Not only that; a draw away at Emirates can be arguably seen as a good result for any team. As my nephew would say, "yes…". However, after being 2-0 up at 60 minutes, anything less than a win must be a disappointment, whatever the circumstances; my nephew again, "…but no".

The team proved not to be completely prepared as of now to confront high pressure challenges for a complete match. LFC seldom had any taste of the ball during 20/25 minutes in the second half. And this LFC team is not ready to stand such pressure by only defending. At certain moments, under Houllier and under Benitez, LFC were able to defend for long periods of time without the ball. But now that is not the case. LFC need to use the football to control the game, and keep it to ease the pressure. And this team has been able to do so against strong oppositions for quite long periods. Against Arsenal, during the first half Arsenal no doubt tried to impose the same high rhythm; however, LFC could manage it and dispute the ball possession.

But that ability was lost in the second half. Leiva, Gerrard and Henderson were unable to keep the ball, to find their team-mates and build solid attacks. And it cannot be argued anything about the opposition physical strength, given that Ramsey/Wilshere were Arsenal midfielders. Leiva is still struggling to be at his level for the whole match, he is only starting to come back after his long spell in the sidelines, and is finding it difficult to be at full strength until the end of the games.

Yes but no. LFC are now to face a game in which its capacity to confront top level matches will be again closely looked at. The players are close to being a real force in the Premier. They need to step up a little bit their consistency and confidence during the games. This next step is proving to be hard. But we are all hoping for a big "yes", without "but no", come Sunday night. Anyway, I will keep enjoying my nephew's idioms, and all his ideas about big rocks and hippopotamuses.

28.- Costly mistakes

Date: 07/02/13
Previous matches: Man City 2-2 LFC (Premier League)

There is a well known saying in chess according to which the winner of a game is the player who make the penultimate mistake. Assuming, of course, that he who makes the last mistake loses the game, that last mistake being definitive. In the match against Man City, LFC made arguably not just the last, but the last two mistakes. As a result, the game was drawn. It was not lost, but given how the match unfolded, it felt as a defeat.

Admittedly with the benefit of hindsight, it is difficult to understand the introduction of Skrtel for Enrique. In his day, Skrtel can do a job playing as a central defender on the right side; but he has proved time and again that he suffers a lot when playing as a central defender on the left side. One occasion that springs to mind is the match against Man City at Anfield, in which it was him who made that costly last mistake playing on the left.

That substitution seemed to be a mistake. There was no apparent reason why Skrtel was particularly needed. Man City were not causing problems, were not playing a type of game especially suited to Skrtel's features. Maybe Enrique, coming back from an injury, needed to leave the pitch; in that case, Wisdom was in the bench for Rodgers to recover a usual defensive line.

In any case, Skrtel cannot play at the left side of the central defence. So one mistake; but not the last. It is true that Skrtel was not to blame for Agüero's goal; that was Reina's mistake, coupled with and excellent action by Agüero himself. That was the last mistake, which decided the final outcome of the match.

A final outcome, a draw away against current Premier League champions, that felt as a defeat, which is massive credit to LFC players and staff. Up until the last stages of the game, it was one of the best games LFC have played in last seasons. LFC were head and shoulders above Man City, in almost every aspect of the game.

Better defence, better built-up game, more control of the game and circulation of the football, more goal chances,…you name it, LFC were better. Even a narrow 2-1 victory sounded harsh for LFC players. They entered the game better, suffered a hard blow in the form of a goal conceded against the run of play, recovered, and achieved the 2-1 through two really magnificent goals.

Then the last mistake and the final 2-2 came. And a bittersweet taste for LFC fans. But there are lots of positives to take from the game, both for the team as a whole and for many players. The team looked composed, in charge of the action, controlling the match, and able to cope with the first goal against. The players kept their game plan, and stamped their authority over Man City players and the game. They kept pushing, did not lose their heads, and looked confident in their own plan and own qualities.

And in doing so they proved to be a better team than Man City, even much better at times. It was not easy, and Man City have great players, who certainly know their work. But overall a great display by LFC team, in a demanding match and in difficult circumstances. An encouraging performance.

Amid a very good general level, several players more than deserve particular praise. Sturridge, Gerrard, Carragher, Leiva stood out. Sturridge, even playing injured for many minutes, was unplayable for City defenders. He seemed to find in every occasion the place where to be to do more harm to the opposition. He kept the football, or run into defenders, or shot at goal, passed the ball, dribbled, and scored a great goal.

Gerrard not only scored another great goal. He masterminded the game, dictated the rhythm, set the pace, and coped with some mistakes in his passes by growing in the match; he was the heart and soul of the team in a very good performance. The introduction of Carragher in defence has added much needed solidity to the team; even Agger has grown with him, either by chance or by Carragher's presence.

Leiva played well for 75/80 minutes. At the end of the match, he started to suffer, most probably due to his recent recovery after a very long injury. He is gradually coming to terms and his game is little by little coming back, but still finds it difficult to stand complete demanding matches. He is improving, though, and did a very good job for the majority of the match.

Yet again, every player did their job, and the team performed very well. It is a shame those mistakes that were so costly. But the team showed to be progressing in good direction. The challenge now is to maintain that level when playing against lesser teams, to keep the focus and motivation. 4th spot remains a distant target, and probably out of reach for this 12/13 season.

Still, the aim should be to end the season as high in the table as possible, and maybe more importantly keep growing in confidence, in consistency, in level of play, keep adjusting, and place the squad in the best possible position ahead of next season, whether 4th spot in finally reachable or not.

Fixtures are apparently on LFC side, with many "winnable" games in coming weeks. But winning winnable games has not been exactly a field of expertise for LFC in recent seasons, so the team needs to keep trying and performing at a good level. As of now, LFC come from a good two away games against Arsenal and Man City; but, just before them, the match against Oldham was very poor. So there is certainly room for optimism; but there is also room for precaution and the necessity of keeping the building process.

Also needed, of course, is avoiding as much as possible those perfectly avoidable mistakes that could ruin great performances, both in football and in chess. It is also known in chess that you might need many good moves to win a mach, but only one bad move to lose it; that is more or less what happened on Sunday. The aim now is to keep those good moves coming.

29.- Football is sometimes...football

Date: 14/02/13
Previous matches: LFC 0-2 WBA (Premier League); Histon U18 0-4 LFC U18 (FA Youth Cup)

Football is sometimes unfair, football is sometimes difficult, football is sometimes a sheer joy, football is sometimes a total despair. Football is all of these, and much more. And LFC are checking it time and again this season, as if it were necessary.

This week alone, and for LFC only, football has been somewhat unfair on occasion of the match against WBA at Anfield. Football has also been almost impossible, given the conditions, on occasion of the LFC win in FA Youth Cup against Histon. All in just three days.

Football was unfair in WBA match. Not grossly unfair, not tremendously unfair, but unfair all the same. LFC, not playing even near its best level, did more than enough to win the game. However, WBA, with nearly nothing to show on the pitch, at least in terms of attacking football, managed to take advantage of two late attacks to bag the win.

That should not disguise the fact that LFC did not play well, did not get close to the level shown again Man City away, or Norwich at Anfield. And that should be something to worry about, not the relative unfairness of the final result. There is nothing to do about the result, but there is much to do, hopefully, regarding the level of LFC game.

Goalkeeper and defenders had little, if anything, to do during almost the whole game. That said, while Johnson added to the attack time and again, and was a constant threat to WBA, Enrique did not go forward as often as one would have expected. It was a shame Johnson was not accurate to profit on all his efforts; as an attacking player, he was almost unstoppable until the final pass, the final cross, or the final shot, which invariably were squandered.

Central defenders and Leiva were also too quiet and shy in their support of the attack, particularly missed in the case of Agger, who can be very useful in midfield and going forward. Whatever the cause, he seldom went to opposition half.

Hence, the attack had to rely on six players (including Johnson). That is a very difficult situation when confronting a stubborn defence. WBA were determined not to allow any space for LFC to attack, and they were defending with the whole team. Still, LFC made things even more difficult for themselves playing only one forward in Suarez.

Football is many things, including a team winning a game in which its utmost aspiration was a draw, as was the case for WBA. But sometimes has also some logic in it. WBA defended with eleven players, LFC attacked with six, five of them in fact closer to midfielders than forwards.

As a result, there were few clear-cut chances. There were a couple of spells in the match in which LFC, when putting together some attacks, created some feeling of the goal coming. And it is also true that a team playing in opposition half as much time as LFC did is likely to win the game. When taking into account the statistics of goal attempts, it is clear that LFC tried hard to win.

And should probably had won; but LFC players did not play particularly well, and the goal attempts were not particularly clear chances. It seems that, having tasted the chance to play with Sturridge up front, the players are now finding it tricky to play without that presence. For whatever reason, Rodgers thought that Borini was not ready to play, and Shelvey and Henderson failed to support Suarez as lone striker.

Downing and Gerrard, along with Johnson, were the ones closer to their real level, and played, if not brilliantly, at least well. But that was not enough. Which was clearly evident when Gerrard missed that penalty, less than fifteen minutes from the end of the match. In all true, that penalty was a harsh decision for WBA, and should probably not have been awarded, but that miss signalled the effective end of the match for LFC and probably the beginning of a new match for WBA, which was able to capitalise.

It was a lesson that points to some room for improvement in LFC, amid this building process the season has become. Being able to effectively attack a close defence is a difficult task in football, and more difficult without real strikers. Surely Rodgers and the staff will keep working to improve that aspect of LFC game.

On the other hand, if there is something the Academy teams have in these days is ability to attack. The players of course face very different challenges in their games than those of the first team, but they keep showing great football. Against Histon in FA Youth Cup Wednesday night, situation was not easy at first sight.

LFC were clearly the team expected to win, but a frozen pitch and a cold night seemed to pose certain challenges to the players. Football was near impossible on that pitch, on that night; however, LFC players were all for it; they stamped their authority on the game in no time from the initial whistle.

Difficult though it was to even stand on their feet, they kept playing as best as they could. And they managed to play some great football in hard conditions. Even after missing a penalty early on, they kept their game plan and ran out comfortable winners, ending the game with a 4-0 victory.

A couple of years ago, the U18 team included Suso, Pacheco, Adojan, Sterling, Ngoo, Morgan, a formidable attacking force full of promises for the future. As of now, some of them are making their progress and getting near or within the first team. Difficult as it is to judge players at this early stage in their careers, it seems that current U18 squad is even better on the attacking side.

Trickett-Smith, Petersen, Gainford, Ibe, Sinclair, Dunn look unstoppable at times; they seem to have everything needed in football, from playmakers to strikers, from central players to wingers. Overall, they seem to be always in the same wavelength when playing, scoring for fun.

Against Histon Gainford did not play, and Ibe was far from his best; Trickett-Smith was in an unknown territory as midfielder. Even so, Trickett-Smith was probably the best player, being everywhere on the field; Petersen was determined to inflict damage to opposition; Dunn was lively in supporting his teammates on the ball, and Sinclair was deadly accurate in his finishing.

These players may, or may not, make it to the first team. But they are a real joy to watch as of now; even in difficult circumstances which prevent them from really delivering, as in the Histon game. Next round is at Anfield, where hopefully they will be closer to their real level.

Football is sometimes tricky, football is sometimes impossible, football is many different things. The now retired football coach Vujadin Boskov was very successful as a coach, but became also very well known for his sentences, many of which have become real common wisdom, real widely known sayings. He once said, after a match difficult to explain, that "football is football". That about sums up everything.

30.- "Know thyself": classic piece of advice and modern day football

Date: 18/02/13
Previous matches: Zenit 2-0 LFC (Uefa Europa League); LFC 5-0 Swansea (Premier League)

A well known classic aphorism, "Know thyself", emphasizes the importance of being aware of both the capacity and limits of oneself. Which is also an important asset in football. Few days ago, manager of Athletic Bilbao Marcelo Bielsa said in a press conference that, of the many mistakes a football team could make, one that is particularly important to avoid is to lose awareness of when they are playing well and when they are playing poorly, to be too blinded by the results and lose track of the real situation.

The moment a manager depicts, in front of his players, a feeling that the team is playing significantly better, or worse, than the players know they are playing, a breach of confidence might occur; the moment the players think that they are playing better, or worse, than they really are, the confusion might appear.

Hence, "know thyself" seems to be a fitting piece of advice for football teams, players and staff. I was reminded of it when reading the reactions of LFC players and staff to the 2-0 defeat against Zenit in Uefa Europa League last Thursday. What caught my attention was to find repeatedly the idea of LFC having played a "perfect match" for about 70 minutes.

On one hand, 70 minutes is not enough, obviously; on the other hand, the match was far from "perfect". It was, maybe, an OK match for 70 minutes, and it is true that the final result was unfairly hard for LFC; but even for those 70 minutes the LFC game was not even close to being perfect.

The game was more or less controlled, and there were some goal chances that could even have decided the round for LFC. At the same time, Zenit had also its chances, and had some amount of control of the game. Any team could have scored the first goal, but the fact is that Zenit did; and, from then on, LFC was unable to really get back to the game and score at least a goal.

All in all, an OK game which could have ended in a draw, or a minimum victory for either side, but which ended in a 2-0 defeat that leaves LFC with a very difficult task for the second leg at Anfield. But to label it anything close to "perfect", even if only the first 70 minutes, is to unnecessarily lower expectations about what is the standard for LFC. Of course, there is always the chance that the perfect match is going to be the second leg at Anfield, and those words are only anticipations.

Not that LFC squad is unaware of what is a good football performance. Few days later, at Anfield against Swansea, the 5-0 victory was a great display of football, of high quality football. It was certainly a match highly influenced by Swansea's preparations for the League Cup final. So, admittedly there was a weakened Swansea side at Anfield. And a side more focussed on next game than on playing against LFC.

Anyway, one can only face the opposition that is present. So LFC needed to confront that Swansea side, not any other. And there were no particularly pleasant circumstances for LFC, either, after a long trip, or a couple of hurting defeats. At the beginning of the match, both teams struggled to handle each other, and the game had no owner for the first moments.

But in few minutes, LFC started to grow on the match, and were steadily approaching that "perfect match" they were unable to play in Russia. Once the pieces start to come together is not easy to identify the initial moment that put all into place. However, there is a widespread feeling that Gerrard was that initial piece.

He settled in midfield and started to dictate the whole game; short passes, tackles, long passes, runs, pressing the opposition,…he did everything. And in almost no time all the players were raising their level and improving the overall performance.

While it was not a perfect match, it was much better than that against Zenit. Against Swansea, the team missed way too many clear-cut chances in the first half. Those potential opening goals are crucial to winning these games, and many chances were squandered, to the extent that the opening needed to come from a penalty that could have been easily avoided by the defender.

Once the first and second goals came, a football storm broke over Swansea defence, and in some moments it seemed as if the goals would come in double figures at the end of the match. The numbers of goal attempts and shots on target were impressive, as was the level of LFC game at times.

On the minus side, to keep the advice of knowing oneself, the pressure to get the football back was not as constant and as intense as one would have expected. LFC defence was inch-perfect in terms of not conceding even the slightest chance of a Swansea goal; but in many occasions the players opted for wait in own half for Swansea to lose the football instead of actively force the mistake of opposition players.

That, of course, is understandable; LFC players have every right to be still recovering from the last, very demanding, string of games, and in fact that tactic was working, so there was no immediate need to change it. But in the long term it will be necessary to improve the press to recover the football earlier.

As said, it doesn't diminish in any sense the great match played at Anfield. Under the guidance of Gerrard, every player clicked in their part. Suarez in particular was ever present, and always linking up and helping the game to progress. One of his finest performances as LFC player, and that is a lot to say. Sturridge is being the perfect player for this team time and again. His mere presence improves the rest of the players. He only needed to be more clinical in front of goal to be unstoppable. His penalty was well deserved, and a nice gesture by his captain to let him take it.

Downing is playing very well, understanding when and where to be to add to the team. He is growing by the game. Coutinho showed some signs of outstanding quality, even if he was clearly not fully ready for the tempo of the game. But if he is able to build on that qualities he can be a great addition; time will tell.

Johnson and Enrique were ready to go forward when appropriate; and of course Enrique scored an absolute beauty, a team effort in which Suarez, Sturridge, Coutinho and him exchanged passes to finally put the ball in the net.

Even the Swansea game was not perfect; but it was much closer to perfection than the Zenit game. And signalled the path LFC need to follow in the work in progress that this season has become. A process in which self-awareness, "Know thyself", will remain important to stay the correct course.

31.- Useless goals

Date: 24/02/13
Previous matches: LFC 3-1 Zenit (Uefa Europa League)

Everything in football goes around goals; how to score them in opposition goal, how to avoid them in own goal. Ultimately, it could be argued that that is precisely to play well. This assertion could, obviously, be to a great extent qualified by several considerations. But goals are definitely important in football.

So much so, that sometimes it leads to bizarre publicly expressed opinions. Few days ago, a Spanish television pundit said, solemnly, that "in these types of games, goals are important". Well, that could hardly be refuted. Goals are, in fact, important, not only in those games, but in every football game. Which is something so true that it is obvious and, in that, irrelevant as a pundit opinion.

However, sometimes goals end up being irrelevant, useless. Once a match finishes in defeat, goals scored seem to have been of little, if any, importance. Even so, in a league competition even those goals in a defeat could prove to be important in the end, should the final position be decided on goal difference.

On the other hand, goals scored in a cup tie that results in being knocked-out are almost surely truly irrelevant. Sometimes, of course, they might serve to boost the confidence of a player or a team, or reward a specific individual performance, or the like, but those goals are almost always truly useless.

In current 12/13 season, one LFC player has become, surely much to his disappointment, a kind of specialist in those useless goals. Joe Allen has, up to now, scored twice for LFC: in the 2-3 FA Cup defeat against Oldham, and in the 3-1 Europa League win against Zenit which meant that LFC went out of the competition.

That means, obviously, nothing against Allen. In fact, both goals could have proven to be the opposite, could have been very important should the team had been able to score once more in any of those games. And in both the team was near, the team had time, and the team was over the opposition. But it wasn't to be.

Against Zenit, LFC came close to getting to the next round, only one goal short at the end of the match, after the task had seemed almost impossible 20 minutes into the match with the first leg result (2-0 defeat) and the Zenit goal. LFC came close, and the players gave no doubt an energetic display. They fought to the end and left everything on the pitch.

However, it was not a good game. Very few clear-cut chances were created, and that elusive 4th goal never really looked like coming. Like he always does, Suarez resisted defeat tirelessly, and scored what seemed a breath of hope, the 3-1 goal, with still plenty of time ahead. Only one goal in the final 30 minutes would have done the trick and would have converted Allen's goal in a very important one.

But there was little inspiration on the pitch. Plenty of fight spirit, plenty of sacrifice, plenty of runs; but little inspiration, little football. The easiness with which LFC have adapted to playing with Sturridge has the other side of showing the difficulties of playing without a striker along Suarez.

It is not (or it is not only) that Suarez himself plays better or worse with another striker or as a lone one. It is also that the team seems to be more able to capitalise on Suarez work when another striker is on the pitch. With the benefit of hindsight, it might have been a good idea to have another forward from the Academy for the Zenit match, at least on the bench.

Allen was one of the players that tried to compensate that absence, and his arriving at the box resulted in his goal, 2-1 at that moment. He has never been prolific in goal scoring, but he has shown a certain eye for goal when allowed to come near the opposition box, both in appearing in dangerous areas and in shooting from distance. He may need to work on that side on his play to grow as a player, but he is showing certain capabilities at that.

Anyway, Allen's help was not enough. Rodgers had been saying since the end of the first leg that the main thing was not an early goal, but the first goal of the match. And that first goal came (from LFC perspective) on the wrong side after Carragher missed a pass to Reina.

It was a shame that an illustrious European career came to an end in that way. Carragher has been everything in LFC defence in many European nights, not to mention domestic ones. But in what was finally his last appearance in international competition it was his mistake what opened the score and made almost impossible for the team to get through.

That mistake, however, should not disguise the fact that Carragher remains a capital piece in LFC defence. In that very match, he managed to recover after the goal and helped his teammates to keep Zenit almost harmless, which is not an easy task. That solidity in defence provided the platform for the team to focus on getting the four goals needed.

Carragher will be sorely missed once he quits playing. But he might have rendered one last service to the club by announcing his retirement. In last transfer windows, a first class central defender has been conspicuous in his absence for LFC. And that has been a weakness of the team. Now, it is imperative to find someone who can play there for LFC; at least one signing for central defence will be needed, and probably even two, if the team wants to aim higher in next season.

Against Zenit, despite not being very inspired, LFC players were able to score three goals, mainly because Suarez's stubbornness and the team spirit and ambition to at least being near the opposition box. That spirit resulted in Allen scoring from the six-yard box, and Suarez converting two free kicks.

Only a little bit more of accuracy by the team would have turned Allen into a hero; Shelvey and Gerrard came close. And the players showed a great spirit, more than matched by the spirit shown by an Anfield crowd that did everything in their power to carry the team to an elusive qualification. Hopefully Allen (and the rest of his teammates) will soon start scoring fully important goals. The Premier League home straight awaits.

32.- Playing anywhere

Date: 26/02/13
Previous matches: LFC U21 0-1 ManU U21 (U21 League)

It is often heard from football players that they would play "anywhere on the pitch" if the team needed them to. And surely they really mean it, even if almost every player must have their own favourite place on the pitch. But for the manager, deploying a player out of position might be a good solution in a given time.

However, playing many players out of position at the same time could be dysfunctional for the team as a whole, as seen in the U21 match between LFC and ManU. In the starting eleven, LFC had two defenders, Wisdom and Sama; two holding midfielders, Coady and Roddan; two forwards, Sterling and Morgan; and four attacking midfielders, Shelvey, Adorjan, Teixeira, and Suso. Well, there was a goalkeeper, too, Ward.

It was a team full of talent, and full of imbalances. Player by player, probably much better than the ManU team. But, as a team, it proved to be inferior. It was not a problem of lacking commitment, of not putting enough effort into the game. It was a case of lacking expertise to playing in those positions; and also a case of players being not accustomed to playing together. Not every player knows how to play in every position, and the team could not fully take advantage of the quality of the players, could not properly function as a team.

During first half, LFC managed to look dangerous in the opposition box in the rare occasion the football reached the attacking players. There was plenty of talent up the field, and it was there to be seen. Problem was that those occasions were rare, and ManU dominated most of the game. Shelvey and Adorjan, as holding midfielders, never really clicked, and ManU players were comfortable in midfield.

In defence, Wisdom, while playing as right back, his usual post this season, looked distracted and not fully focused; at left back, Roddan really struggled in an unknown position. He fought hard, and managed to more or less control the opposition attacks, but was unable to help when in possession.

Up on the pitch, Teixeira looked lively, inspired, and always comfortable on the ball and able to cause damage; Sterling tried his runs, and threatened to inflict harm; on the other hand, both Morgan and Suso were not really having their best day, and could not add to the team efforts in attack.

The team looked unbalanced and had a hard first half; when called into action, it must be said, Sama and Coady as centre-backs and Ward as a goalkeeper were excellent and played a major part in reaching half time with 0-0 in the score sheet.

Things were going to get worse few minutes into the second half, when Sama was sent off, and the team became even more of a jigsaw; Wisdom, now the only defender, moved to centre-back and Shelvey to right back. Teixeira joined Adorjan in the middle, and Morgan and Sterling swapped positions in a wise move aiming at playing a very quick player up front.

Predictably enough, it took time for the players to adapt to the new, even more difficult, circumstances. A ManU goal looked like coming for a while, but the lack of accuracy by ManU forwards, the fight and effort by LFC players, the rock-solid performance by Coady, and the actions by Ward were enough to keep the clean sheet.

In time, LFC started to even threaten ManU goal; Shelvey, who had had an indifferent game to that moment, started to play not just out of position; in fact, he started to play in various positions at the same time. He was right back when defending; holding midfielder in keeping hold of the football, and playmaker on the attack, all in one player. He delivered some excellent passes, bringing attacking players into the game. He looked very comfortable playing all those roles at once.

Teixeira continued to look composed and assured as well as inspired, Sterling kept being lively, and even Suso improved his game, only Morgan failing to came into terms with the game. Hence, LFC were little by little levelling the game; always spending more time defending than attacking, but with some chances in the opposition box.

Getting close to the end of the match, it seemed that the worse moments had been left behind. That is, only seemed, because with almost the last kick of the match ManU scored their only goal to finish the game 1-0 winners. A very hard ending for LFC players, who gave everything they could to keep the result. And an especially harsh ending for LFC goalkeeper Ward, who even in that last action had been excellent only to see a ManU player placing the last rebound into the net.

All in all, the defeat can hardly be deemed as unfair. ManU were a better team on the night, it had more goal chances, and probably deserved the win. From LFC point of view, however, it was hard that the defeat came that way, in the nick of time, after so much effort put into the pitch, after so difficult circumstances in the team sheet.

The players worked their socks off and tried their best. But it is not an easy task to perform in an unfamiliar role surrounded by new players. Roddan, Shelvey, or Adorjan were only a fraction of the players they usually are. Sterling, Sama, or Teixeira, in more familiar roles, played well but struggled to make an impact in the game. Wisdom, Morgan and Suso, even in known positions, were not at their best. And the team as a whole found it difficult to adjust and deliver.

Finally, Coady, out of position, and goalkeeper Ward, in his very well known position, were both excellent; so much so that it might have raised questions about whether Coady should play more often as centre-back. Only time will tell.

But there is little doubt that it is one thing to play the odd player out of position and it is a completely different thing to play half a team out of position. Which brings into attention, once more, the schedule and organization of youngster football competitions. LFC have many games (U18, U19, U21, Youth Cup) in few days, and many players, who would have improved the team, were, rightfully, rested against ManU.

On the other side, the experience may add to the formation process of the players involved. They may discover new abilities or weaknesses that could be useful when growing up to become fully formed players. What is wrong in the short term may sometimes be right in the long term, and developing new skills can do no harm to the formation of the players; LFC may end up benefiting from these types of games, from playing the players all around the pitch.

33.- Big players making themselves count

Date: 03/03/13
Previous matches: Wigan 0-4 LFC (Premier League)

An old, unresolved, and in all likelihood never to be solved, dispute in football is about the extent to which results, goals, and football performances are determined by the quality of players involved and to what extent the organizing skills and wisdom by managers are the main key to that same football success.

So, it was Guardiola's Barça excellence an easy task and a foregone conclusion given the quality of the players? Or did the players look particularly good because of Guardiola' excellence as manager? Is it an easy job to manage the Spanish national football team now? Or is Del Bosque a great manager because he gets his players to play as they do? Does Ferguson's success come primarily from his accuracy in choosing players to sign, or even from the money he has at his disposal? Or are his qualities as manager the main factor?

Needless to say, there is not an absolute extreme in the question. A team full of talent with no organization or tactical work at all will likely achieve little success; a team with lots of organization but built with non talented players will go little distance. Hence, both quality and tactical awareness are needed, and an appropriate balance has to be found between them. But the debate will continue as to how much importance bears each of the factors.

In this endless debate, the 4-0 victory of LFC against Wigan meant a point scored for the importance of the sheer talent of the players. In all likelihood, the same match, with the same game plan by the managers, but with Suarez and Coutinho wearing the shirt of Wigan, would have ended up in a totally different final score.

That is not to diminish in the slightest the involvement of Rodgers or of other LFC players, but to single out the outstanding performance by those extremely gifted players. LFC played undoubtedly a good match, and fully deserved the win, even if probably the margin was too harsh for Wigan, and not a fully fair reflection of what happened on the pitch.

For once, everything went in favour of LFC, from scoring quickly in the match to managing to prevent Wigan to come close in the score sheet in defining moments. The level of performance by Suarez was hardly surprising, given the level he has maintained all season; still, even if hardly surprising, he almost always finds a way to astonish. In this match, he was inch-perfect in converting his goal chances.

His first goal was pure class, in the way he sent the goalkeeper the wrong place before softly placing the ball in the net; his third goal was pure determination, will to score, resolution to see the ball into the goal. And his second goal…well, the definite prove, if needed, that this man can do no wrong as of now. In taking the free kick he slipped to the ground, and still the football managed to find its way to Wigan goal.

But, as said, Suarez is expected to perform such things. Coutinho, on the other hand, is still unknown to many LFC fans. But what he has shown to date is extremely promising. Against Swansea, even if he scored, he looked classy but out of rhythm and struggling to take part in the game. Against Wigan he took the match by storm in the first minutes.

He was unplayable for Wigan defenders during those first minutes, and dictated the game almost at will. The best way to prevent the rhythm of the game to outplay you is to dictate the rhythm personally; and that was what Coutinho did at the beginning of the match. That attitude reflected on the score in the two first and defining goals, in which Coutinho provided the decisive assist.

Later in the match, he showed that, as he himself has pointed out, he is not fully prepared, physically, to cope with a Premier League game for ninety minutes. But Rodgers is well aware of that and he is gradually adding to the minutes Coutinho spends on the field. Which is favoured, of course, by the fact that in these two first games started by Coutinho the result was decided way before the final whistle.

Along with Suarez and Coutinho there was another decisive LFC player. It may seem strange to say that the goalkeeper played a big part when the game ended in a 4-0 win, but in this case that is true. Reina made some terrific saves which helped to keep the score when Wigan could still harbour hopes of getting something from the game, and even made his (huge) contribution in the first goal, with a great long pass.

While generally speaking it is not a good sign that the goalkeeper is instrumental, in this case it is very good news for LFC. Reina is having a difficult season, and has indeed not consistently reached his best level for the last couple of seasons. And, on the long term, a good goalkeeper is an essential piece of every successful football team.

To finish this season on a high, LFC will need Reina to step up his level, and this match could provide him with a platform to do so. He looked sharp, focused, and confident. He looked close to his best. If he can keep improving in the next games, and overall maintain a consistently high level, it would enormously add to LFC chances of a good season finish.

On the minus side, Allen is still struggling to find his form. He looked out of pace, out of rhythm, and not knowing where he was needed in the team. He could not dictate the game from midfield, and was not the player he was at the beginning of the season. He will need to find back his best form.

The rest of the team played well; Johnson did not go into the attack as often as usual, but his action in the last goal was pure class; Enrique went more often into the attack, even if he was not particularly decisive. Carragher and Agger coped well with a crowded Wigan attack, and answered the majority of questions directed at them by Wigan's players.

Leiva, Gerrard and Downing did their jobs. None of them was particularly brilliant, even if Downing opened the score, but all of them did their bits. It is not a bad note for a team, being able to comfortably win a match with no need of every player performing at their best.

It was, overall, a professional display by LFC players capped by three brilliant performances by Coutinho, Reina, and Suarez. A solid team, even if it might have lacked a bit of ambition to keep on scoring in the second half. Hopefully the players are saving their goals for the visit of Tottenham next Sunday, in a potentially highly demanding match.

A professional display in which the excellence of certain players decided the game. Surely Rodgers would be happy to be in little time in the situation of Guardiola or Del Bosque, with football fans wondering whether he is that good, or his players are the real stars. That would be great for LFC.

34.- Winning wings

Date: 06/03/13
Previous matches: LFC U18 3-1 Leeds U18 (FA Youth Cup)

Fortunately, in football there are many ways by which one team can become a success. In both senses: many ways to be a success in the long term, and many ways to win a particular match.

Those many ways allow for the enrichment of football debates, which might offer many nuances, and which are difficult to close with a definitive reason. One such definitive reason could have been that of Alf Ramsey, who led England to World Cup success with what was called "The Wingless Wonders", that is, a team which played with no proper wings in favour of playing more players through the middle of the pitch.

For those tactics to come and be successful in a national team usually known for his long and fruitful tradition of wingers could have proven to be decisive in stating that wings were surplus to requirements in football. Nearly fifty years after, such statement is by no means universally accepted.

Successful teams have come and gone, both with and without wings. Even more, other forms to use the sides of the pitch have been put in place by different managers, from the so called "total football" in the 70's, in which almost any player could appear in the wings at any given moment, to the "long full backs" in the 90's in which teams deploying three centre-backs allowed the full backs to be particularly attacking. Or forwards appearing on the wings, or midfielders going into attack through the wings, and so on.

However, a solution that should not be forgotten is...proper wingers playing in the wings. That can also be a winning formula, providing of course the wingers have the required quality, which is not very usual nowadays.

One such formula, with remarkable success, could be seen during the 3-1 win by LFC against Leeds in FA Youth Cup. LFC played Dunn at right wing and Ibe at left wing, and both players were head and shoulders over their team mates, and were instrumental in the victory. It was one of that satisfying occasions in which winning goal scorers were exactly the best players on the night.

A night in which LFC were not very inspired, were not at their best, and for relatively long spells were dominated by Leeds. In fact, in certain sense it could be argued that, as a team, Leeds were somewhat better. However, the wings made the difference in the match, much to LFC fortune.

Dunn and Ibe run, dribbled, pass, and scored almost at will, inflicting great damage to opposition defence. Both proved to be not only better players than the rest on the pitch, but to be better players by a great margin, to be in a different class. It was perfectly appropriate that they both scored on the night.

On the other hand, elsewhere on the team, LFC players were not at their best. Sinclair seldom found how to really get close to scoring; Baio and Maguire, as full backs, were very quiet in attack, although they managed to be strong in defence. Lussey and Rossiter were second best to Leeds midfielders.

Of course, Rossiter is much younger, and was probably playing his greater game to date. All circumstances taken into account, he gave a good account of himself and was firm on the pitch. All credit to him for his effort, but from the football point of view, Leeds midfielders were better.

Centre-backs played better. Jones has made tremendous progression this season, and looks more and more comfortable by the game. He has an imposing presence, and knows how to use his physical qualities in his game as centre-back. He is learning his craft and getting to know the job of a centre-back, a position in which experience is very important.

And Brewitt was very good news for LFC. Extremely young and hence inexperienced, he never looked out of pace, out of position, or lost on the pitch. He offered an outstanding work on the night and the team benefited from his presence. Both centre-backs provided the team with much needed solidity in a game that in which LFC did not dominate or dictate the rhythm.

At goal, keeper Fulton was generally right in his actions, though he showed some doubts and some unusual mistakes for his quality. In a very different position, something similar happened to Trickett-Smith, who despite some good appearances was not regular on the night and struggled at times.

In a below par performance by the team, the wings proved to be the silver bullet. Leeds were probably left wondering what else could they have done to win the match; but what is clear is that its defenders were unable to cope with Ibe and Dunn. Not for the first time in the season, Ibe in particular seemed to be far superior to his opponents, and as likely as not will need to be sooner than later played along, and against, older players to keep improving and fulfil his potential.

In a slightly inferior level, Dunn was also great, and showed encouraging signs for the future. He is trying to complete his come back after a while on the sidelines, and his improvement is evident in last matches.

Overall, both proved that wings, occupied by proper wingers, can also be a winning weapon in football. There are many potentially winning formulas in football, and the key for a manager is to find the one that is best suited to the traits of the players at his disposal. That is probably the real winning formula, to get the most from the players.

In 1966 Ramsey had at hand outstanding wingers, including LFC's Thompson, yet he decided to go with his "Wingless Wonders". And that proved to be a good decision, given that England won the World Cup. Nobody could tell whether a team with wingers would have also won.

Against Leeds in the FA Youth Cup, LFC trusted its wingers; and that was also a great decision, a winning decision. Having defining wingers in the team will always be a good asset that could be eventually put to good use. Ibe and Dunn are, as of now, very promising for LFC.

35.- Ongoing lessons

Date: 13/03/13
Previous matches: Hull U18 0-3 LFC U18 (FA Youth Cup)

Youth football is, and have always been, about nurturing young players through their learning process to allow them to achieve their full potential; or, at least, as much of it as possible. When it comes to youth football in elite clubs, that potential aims to be reflected in getting into the first team. If that proves to be not possible, getting as higher as possible within the potential of each player.

That is, looking at the footballing side of it. There are of course other aspects regarding aiding to the fulfilment of personal development through football experience, in which football is more a means and not an end. But when looking at the football aspect of it, youth football is about getting the most of the football ability of those engaged in youth football and its process.

This process involves helping the players to grow in all different factors related to football, it being technical, tactical, physical, mental, and so on. One of last aspects to learn is that of learning to properly play highly demanding football matches. Competing against determined rivals, knowing when and where to act; when to pass or when to dribble; where to run with the ball, where to look for a teammate; when to shoot at goal or when to give that extra pass; where to keep the ball and where to play a long ball; and many more others whens and wheres that will ultimately determine the football fate of many players.

LFC U18 team had one hard lesson of these types of when and where, of that necessary learning, in the FA Youth Cup match against Hull. An all important quarter-final, played in Hull's soil. And LFC players showed to have learnt well in the Academy, and to have taken good advantage of the lessons they are being taught.

If in the previous FA Youth Cup round, at Anfield against Leeds Utd., LFC won the game through a solid defensive display combined with two excelling wingers, Hull provided an entirely different challenge. Hull players packed in their own half, played tight and narrow, never fought for the possession, and offered a defensive performance waiting for the odd goal chance that almost inevitably arises sooner or later in every football match.

A tactic that one could say that worked almost to perfection in the first half, in which the football was at LFC feet but in which Hull had as many goal chances as LFC. LFC players were confronted with a challenge that might be a valuable lesson for their football careers. A challenge to face a packed defence and find ways to break it to create goal chances. That is something LFC players will hopefully need to do in years to come, and something not very usual in youngsters' football, where players are not ready to play such type of defence.

And it must be said that Hull players performed very well for long spells. In particular, during the first half in which they managed to frustrate LFC players time and again. LFC played fairly well, but not well enough to score, and not even well enough to deserve to score. Players moved the football around Hull box, tried to find weaknesses in Hull defence, kept the possession, got to wide areas, found the wingers, and did everything to the manual.

Maybe even too much to the manual in that their game became predictable and little space was really found. In fact, it might be argued that Hull were closer to score than LFC. Even so, LFC effort has to be praised. Players had had little experience of such a match, and they tired tirelessly to play as they should. They lacked some energy, some improvisation, some edge. But they dominated the whole first half and kept their focus, never allowing easy Hull counterattacks. It was a case of them perfecting their craft, their defence-demolition abilities.

Defence-demolition that came in the second half. The problem with such defending displays is that the team could do it to perfection and, even so, a little distraction, a rebound, a set-piece, might end up in a goal, with devastating effects. And that was exactly what happened in the match; little before 10th minute in the second half, score was 0-0; little after that 10th minute, score was 2-0 for LFC.

Firstly, a clever set-piece situation by LFC ended up in centre-back Jones slamming the ball into the Hull net and opening the score; few minutes later, Jones himself delivered a great long pass to Dunn that resulted in 2-0. In almost no time Hull defence had been outplayed and LFC's patience and determination had had its reward.

From then on, LFC managed the game superbly, allowing no space for Hull to even think of coming back into the match. At the end, Dunn even scored again to make it 3-0, but the match had been decided long before, in what was a demanding exercise for LFC players, very well solved.

In a very difficult game, against a side that prevented Dunn and Ibe from having the kind of influence they, and the team, are used to, LFC fought to find other ways, found those ways, and kept the match under control. After some initial problems, adjustments were made and Hull were seldom a threat to LFC goal. Keeping the match under control allowed LFC players to keep on looking for the opening goal.

It was difficult, and LFC players were not at their best; but, even so, as a team they proved to be very mature for that age. Lussey and Rossiter offered a very convincing performance in midfield, dictating the tempo and stopping Hull's attempts of getting in LFC half. Defenders were always focused and ready to help midfielders in managing the football. Dunn, and particularly Ibe, instead of getting frustrated by the difficulties, kept trying, even if they were not as inspired as usual. Trickett-Smith found it hard to face Hull defence, and was not as brilliant as in other matches; Sinclair worked endlessly and kept defenders worried in a lacklustre yet effective display.

The whole team had a difficult game up until the goals. They had almost no space or time to play, they were often frustrated by defenders, they were not at their best; but they kept trying, they kept looking for the opener and kept the control of the match. And, in doing so, they added another valuable lesson to their baggage. They are better footballers today for having experienced such challenges yesterday.

And they are through in the FA Youth Cup. Winning trophies is not the main target at youth football, but it makes the process more pleasant, more rewarding, and helps to be in a good mood in training ground. Amidst everything one needs to learn to become a professional footballer, it is of no little relevance that of learning how to win, and LFC U18 players advanced in that lesson during this game.

36.- Self-awareness

Date: 16/03/13
Previous matches: LFC 3-2 Tottenham (Premier League)

After the victory against Tottenham at Anfield, LFC were left in a very good mood, with good feelings to face the last games of the season, and with certain hope of getting into the top five, or four, still remaining.

It was, moreover, a victory after coming from behind, which is always particularly satisfactory for fans, players, and staff, in that that kind of victory shows not only footballing ability but also the type of mental strength that is needed to achieve great things in football.

Hence, there was some very good news for LFC as a result of that game. The team continued with its late string of good results, kept its recently found goal profligacy, got its first win of the season against one of the top teams, and extended for another week the dream of a really good end of season.

It all being true, it should not be forgotten, however, that it was not a particularly well played football match by LFC. Self-awareness is important to keep growing. And self-awareness is most likely very much in place inside Anfield and Melwood. For long spells in the match, LFC were totally outplayed by an average Tottenham team.

A Tottenham team that were far from its best, too. But, even so, managed to dominate the game for long periods.

In fact, first and second LFC goals came against the run of the game, with only the third one more or less a result of the situation on the pitch. That has, clearly enough, two very different interpretations, both of them very valid.

On one hand, it could be argued that the team played below its level over last matches, but still managed to win a very difficult match, which is a sign of a mature and resilient team; on the other hand, it might be stressed that, despite the victory, the reality is that the team played far from its own standards, which could be a bad sign for coming games.

As said above, both of them are true and valid approaches, one of them stressing the positive of the victory, one of them insisting on the negative of a below par performance. In their public comments, every LFC player and coach, including the manager, have opted for the positive approach; inside the dressing rooms, they are probably working with a more balanced approach.

It is very well to celebrate the successes and thus reinforce the team; and this win was clearly a success; but self-awareness should also be there to calibrate the euphoria and have the squad working to correct the mistakes and improve. That balanced assessment would help the team to keep the confidence arising from winning a difficult match while at the same time keeping up the good work to improve the level of game for future matches.

That self-awareness has been already proved by Rodgers during the season. And it was proved again in a pivotal moment of the Spurs match. In the middle of the second half the score was 2-1 to Tottenham, and the match looked all but decided. Central midfielders Parker and Livermore, with the help of Dembele, were absolutely winning the midfield fight against Leiva and Gerrard; as a result, the match was being dominated by Spurs, the rhythm was being dictated by Spurs; and only a good defensive performance by LFC, along with some poor playing by Spurs players, were keeping the score at 2-1.

At that very moment, in which many fans, but I would also say many managers, too, would have made a substitution involving introducing an attacking player, Rodgers decided for the opposite. In what was a bold, but ultimately right, movement, Allen went on, Coutinho went out. With hindsight, it seems almost obvious; but I don't think it was at the moment.

But Rodgers saw it right: LFC were losing the midfield battle, so what was needed was another midfielder; and LFC had on the pitch enough attacking force to hurt opposition defence. It is difficult to say to what extent that substitution was really decisive. Maybe everything would have happened the same way without that change; in the end, after all, second LFC goal came through a great defensive mistake.

But with Allen on the pitch LFC were better equipped to fight Spurs midfield, which allowed the players to defend higher up on the pitch, which in turn might have been pivotal in that mistake. Or maybe it was just pure chance. But from that moment LFC looked more comfortable on the pitch, got the game to Spurs half, and finally, with no little dose of luck, achieved victory.

Self-awareness, being conscious of where are the weaknesses at a given moment, spotting the key point of the game, all of it played a big part in the victory. That same self-awareness should single out some specifics in the somewhat weak performances of some players. Johnson and Enrique were way much restricted to defence; one of the rare occasions in which Enrique came into attack gave way to the opener, but that happened in few moments; Leiva couldn't stand the challenge by Spurs midfield.

But there were two different players playing way below their usual level. Agger was repeatedly caught out of position, and watched from close distance how Vertonghen caused havoc in LFC box; Sturridge didn't find his place in the match. He never was particularly dangerous, and failed to have good understanding with the rest of LFC attacking players.

Sturridge has been great since his arrival, and this first below par performance ended with an important win by the team. However, LFC will need an improved version of Sturridge, that that has been seen to date, if the season is to end up on a high. Also needed will be Coutinho, who kept his adjustment to the Premier process, with some good movements and actions.

The fact that his substitution coincided with a marked improvement in the score sheet had probably little to do with Coutinho's own performance in the match, and much to do, as said before, with a structural problem in the midfield, that was adequately corrected by Rodgers, thanks to that self-awareness., that might be of great help in the continuous process of growing and building of the team.

37.- Resigning, retiring

Date: 20/03/13
Previous matches: Southampton 3-1 LFC (Premier League)

Over last month there has been a great deal of talking about the resignation of former Pope Benedict XVI. His decision prompted a debate about what are the implications of resigning from a very especial position, and, more interestingly, a debate about to what extent the very conditions in which he felt in that position determined that resignation. In particular, the decisions and changes which are to be taken and made in the organization (in his case, Catholic Church) in relation with such resignation. For some experts, in a sense, it was like shedding light on the real situation in Rome and reforms needed there.

On the other hand, other pundits have simply seen that decision as a retirement, more than a resignation. In their view, an old and tired man has done everything within his power, and decided to step aside and allow for others to step in. So there would have been nothing particularly drastic, or dramatic, about it, and no need for any particular changes within the organization as a whole.

Recently, LFC have had its own long time servant announcing his retirement, him being of course Jamie Carragher. With his history at the club, he is not one player like any other, and his retirement is something of a resigning, in a sense; a very honourable one, and fully understandable at that. From his personal point of view, it might well be the case that he simply feels no longer ready to keep on challenging for his position in the starting eleven, and has decided to begin another stage in his career. No one could blame him for that, having been at the club for over a quarter century by now.

Even so, whether it was deliberate or not, his retirement exposes even more obviously a weakness in the squad that has been proving to be costly for years, that of central defenders. LFC have an illustrious past in central defenders, and in recent times Hyyppia and Carragher formed a formidable force there; with the addition of Agger, that flank were exceedingly well covered.

However, as of now, and after many attempts by successive managers, there are no adequate replacements for them. Fortunately enough, Agger have stayed injury free this season, and Carragher, when finally called into action, has been performing well, even if far from his best of some years ago.

And that is it. Skrtel is not even near the level required for LFC; and Coates, the other resource there, appears not to have the confidence of the staff. Wilson has been loaned out. And other seemingly promising centre backs like Kelly and Wisdom have been deployed as right backs. Decisive action will need to be taken on this front in next transfer window. Whether or not Coates is able to occupy that place is something only the coaches that see him in training day in day out will know, although signs are not very promising as of now.

Without a solid platform in central defence there is no way a team can sustain a consistent run of games, which is needed to do well in long league competitions. It is unlikely a coincidence that ManU, the more consistent team, the more able to win games without playing particularly well, enjoy the best combination of central defenders in Ferdinand, Vidic, Evans, Smalling, or Jones. A combination that has been able to endure the long absence of Vidic, or the physical problems of Ferdinand. In the long term, solid centre backs are the safeguards that make it possible for a team to navigate a poor string of performances.

That is not to deny the importance of goalkeepers, full backs, midfielders or forwards; that is to stress the importance of centre backs, particularly in league competitions. And to stress the current weakness of LFC on that front. A weakness that the retirement of Carragher has put on the front line, if it was needed.

In the game against Southampton, LFC had a generally speaking below par performance, all around the team. But goals conceded were very soft goals; first and third goals involved long runs by Southampton players in front of LFC defenders, Skrtel in particular, that were unable to prevent them from scoring. Second goal, after a deflected free kick, was mainly due to bad luck, and a mistake from Suarez in the wall; but the foul was a result of Skrtel disputing a ball and not winning it even with the foul.

Needless to say, Skrtel was not the only responsible for the defeat; not even near. Football is a team effort, and all players on the pitch lose and win together. The defeat, and team display, simply showed the difficulties LFC are having in that sector of the pitch.

And not only in that sector. Under Rodgers, LFC seem to be trying to play controlling the game, dictating the rhythm, owning the ball possession. However, that is only achieved with enough midfielders on the pitch, either proper midfielders or players that play there during the match.

In last games, team has lost its balance, and Gerrard, Leiva or Allen are finding themselves isolated in midfield, with insufficient support there. Downing and Coutinho play close to the wings and advanced on the pitch, not providing direct help in midfield. Suarez and Sturridge have more than enough tasks looking for spaces in attack. Johnson and Enrique are either in defence or directly in attack, leaving the midfield empty. As a result, there is no means for LFC to effectively control the game and ball possession.

Hence, if and when players manage to get the football into attacking positions, the team is able to look dangerous, create goal chances and eventually score goals. But defenders are often exposed to opposition players arriving at positions near LFC box; and then the defence is not strong enough to stand the attacks.

In that aspect of midfield, problem is not so much a lack of players, as in central defence, as a lack of correspondence between the game plan and the players on the pitch. Here, there are solutions in the squad. While not the best players in the world, Henderson, Shelvey, or Suso could help in midfield, if needed. And when Leiva, Gerrard and Allen played together against Tottenham the team played better.

Or Rodgers can stick to his starting eleven with Downing, Coutinho, Suarez and Sturridge, which is no doubt a threatening attacking force; but in that case the game plan should change and adjust a little bit to effectively confront opposition teams like Southampton.

Either way, the central defence weakness shown by both the Southampton game and the retirement of Carragher will need to be addressed in summer. Benedict XVI has already his replacement in Pope Francis, a football fan in fact; an inspired Carragher's replacement will be crucial to LFC standing a chance to be successful next season.

38.- Slow and steady progress

05/04/2013
Previous matches: Aston Villa 1-2 LFC (Premier League)

After so many years since last league title, LFC is still in the process of learning how to win leagues. In past seasons, there have been some weak LFC squads, but also, now and then, some very good squads, potentially capable of achieving league success.

Those seasons have not been completely unsuccessful for LFC, which have achieved almost every title except the Premier League: FA Cup, League Cup, Uefa Cup and even Champions League. Only Club World Cup and Premier League have eluded LFC during these years.

However, Premier League is as of now a great source of frustration for LFC as a club and LFC fans. Some seasons the team has looked good enough to win, and indeed the amount of titles achieved speaks of a consistently good team; but, for one reason or another, it has been impossible to win the league, and even to perform well in it, with only a couple of 2nd places in league tables in last 20 years.

One aspect of league winning that has proved to be particularly tricky for LFC squads is that of making the quality of its players count in obscure matches, against lesser teams, in uninspired performances. That is a quality in which ManU have excelled in last seasons, in which even Man City, Chelsea or Arsenal have been successful to a certain extent. And a feature LFC need to improve on if league success is to be achieved.

Now, I am not speaking of "winning ugly", of winning undeserved matches, playing poorly; which is, of course, a highly rewarding ability. What I am referring to is the ability to deserve the win in matches not particularly well played, thanks mainly to the superior quality of the players.

A superior quality that allows the defenders to frustrate the opposition and keep clean sheets (or, at least, get few goals against); and that allows the forwards to convert goal chances into goals at high conversion rates.

That is an ability that has been difficult to show for LFC squad for years. And an ability in which LFC seems to be improving on during this season. Slow improvement, no doubt, with setbacks; but improvement, nonetheless. An improvement that in last game against Villa was there to be seen in two particular aspects: on one hand, it is always more difficult to win such games in opposition grounds; on the other hand, for the first time in the season, LFC recovered from starting behind in the score to win the match.

And while the game was far from perfect, the win was well deserved. That was a step in the good direction. Not the finished article, but another brick in the building process. Up until now, LFC have, time and again, squandered such improvements in subsequent matches, but maybe this time it will be different.

One thing needed in winning these types of matches is to more players to claim the spotlight; a team cannot rely on a few players to decisively perform in every game. And against Villa some individual performances showed improvement.

Henderson not only scored the all important first goal, but also, after a weak beginning of the game, added solidity to midfield, and to the team; Johnson went into attack more often, and more sharply, than during past matches; Reina was close to his best, and had a couple of defining saves; Carragher and Agger, though not brilliant, were able to reasonably cope with the challenges posed by Benteke.

Enrique and Leiva did more or less OK, whereas Downing had a below par match, maybe influenced by his past with Villa. Gerrard, Suarez and particularly Coutinho were close to their usual high standards, and tormented Villa defenders during the match.

Tactically, Rodgers reacted to bad signs of late reinforcing the midfield with Henderson in the place of Sturridge. While not the ideal solution, it proved to be a wise move in the day. LFC had been struggling lately for lack of control in midfield, and Sturridge had lost some of his initial prowess. So that Rodgers movement made sense not only during the match, but also before the match.

And it worked well. That decision improved the capacity of controlling the football, and thus the game, in midfield, and also the capacity to defend when Villa got the control. It was enough to convincingly win the Villa game, in which solidity, control, and some drops of brilliance in attack were the key to victory.

In the long term, and against stronger teams, it will most likely be necessary to find a way to bring Sturridge back to the team. As of now, Downing seems to be the likely choice to lose his place in the starting eleven, although other possibilities will be arising depending on the moment, and on the rival.

An increasingly decisive piece of the team, Coutinho seems to be able to provide the spark, the inspiration, the final pass, that the team has so much missed in past seasons. To be a real force and not only a brilliant but irregular asset, he will need to adjust his game to the Premier League rhythm, improve his physically, and win consistency; hopefully it all will be slowly, but steadily, coming to Coutinho performances.

Slow and steady progress and improvement that the team also needs. Villa game was a short step in the right direction, being able to win games in which the team is better than the opposition but not really convincing in its game. Many more other aspects need to be added before the team becomes a real challenger for the title. The final games of this season will determine whether the club goes into next season with confidence in the progress made and success to come.

39.- Aphorisms and football wisdom

Date: 12/04/13
Previous matches: LFC 0-0 West Ham (Premier League); LFC U21 3-2 Arsenal U21 (U21 League)

It being a popular cultural expression, it is not surprising football that has originated, or adapted, many aphorisms to explain its circumstances. As nearly every aphorism in life, football aphorisms end up being accurate sometimes and inaccurate other times. Even so, those aphorisms can be, and in fact are, held as absolute truth in the occasions in which they are proven right; or as conventional wisdom in lots of conversations; but they tend to stand and be recurrently referred to even if they are proven wrong in certain occasions.

Those football aphorisms reflect, so to speak, a conventional wisdom about the game; only that they can be contradictory at times, and sometimes it seems as if for each different idea you could find an aphorism to back your view. In that sense, football aphorisms are, of course, no different from other aphorisms in other aspects of life, and they can both illuminate and obscure any argument.

One very popular football aphorism is "never change a winning team", more or less the football reflection of "if it is not broken, do not fix it". In modern day football, it is difficult to test the accuracy of the aphorism. It is increasingly difficult to see an unchanged starting eleven from one match to another. Injuries, suspensions, prevention, rotation, tactical considerations,…all of them add to the managers pondering, and effecting, changes from week to week, from match to match.

Long gone are the Shankly days of the 60's, in which the players on the pitch were almost invariably the same week in week out, and in which a title winning squad could consist in only fourteen or fifteen players. Even in the 80's, a Spanish team, Athletic Bilbao, famously won the title using barely fourteen players in all league season (the rest of the squad playing only the odd game).

But it is not impossible to witness an unchanged team even nowadays; and frequently it is indeed a winning team. Case in point, LFC against West Ham. Rodgers, with LFC coming from a convincing victory against Villa, opted for keeping his faith in the same starting eleven to play West Ham.

With the benefit of hindsight, it might be considered not a good idea. However, at the moment, few would have argued with the decision. After the January transfer window the team-sheet has been step by step consolidating, and the changes have been few, with the general structure well in place. Hence, it was possibly only a matter of time that the staff named an unchanged team.

Probably the only change that maybe could have made sense was that of Sturridge in the place of Downing. And, as minutes passed, that was exactly the substitution that Rodgers had to make before 30 minutes because of Downing having a bout of sick. So, in a sense, we had the privilege of seeing, in one match, both alternatives, the unchanged team and the team with the most likely change.

Neither of those really worked. LFC never really found the spark needed for a fully attacking match, nor the continuity or consistency necessary to open the score sheet and achieve a victory. Not that the team played particularly poorly, or that the players lacked ambition, or commitment; but it was seen from nearly the beginning of the match that they were not at their very best.

There were some goal chances, and with only a bit of luck the match could have ended with an LFC victory (equally as true, a little more of bad luck, and the match would have ended with a West Ham victory). Anyway, LFC were the most likely team to win on the day, but it was not a fully convincing display. Once again, the team failed to build a momentum with consecutive victories. All in all, an unchanging winning team was not the winning formula in this occasion.

One league in which there is no point in even thinking of displaying an unchanged team is the U21s. Here, to all the factors involved in senior teams one have to add the tricky schedules, players on loan, or international matches, among the reasons that make almost impossible to repeat teams, either winning or losing. It is not completely impossible, but very difficult, much more so than in senior competitions.

Academy football has its own conventional wisdom, regarding the potential of players, and how to spot it. One disputed question is that of the goalkeepers. Generally speaking, one could talk of two different sets of qualities that make a good goalkeeper. On one hand the reliability, the capacity of not conceding obviously avoidable goals; on the other hand, what one could consider the geniality, the ability to avoid goals that no one could blame the goalkeeper for conceding.

Needless to say, the ultimate goalkeeper would gather both capacities; and certainly no goalkeeper is totally reliable, nor a total genius. Everyone can claim to have both qualities to an extent. However, it is not easy to decide which set of qualities are preferable for a goalkeeper. LFC wise, Clemence was probably more reliable, Grobbelar more genial, both great goalkeepers.

When speaking of youngsters, what should a goalie scout look for? Arguably, it will depend on the type of team. For the vast majority of teams, reliability is probably more important. As Di Stefano, then Real Madrid manager, once said to one of his keepers, "you may not save the shoots on target, but please don't divert into the net a shoot off target".

However, for title challenging teams, it is probably worth sometimes to let go some reliability in exchange for some points-winning geniality. One such points winning goalkeepers seems to be in LFC Academy now. Danny Ward has displayed this season some outstanding performances, and is becoming a regular with the U21s.

Some of his brilliance was shown in the U21s league victory against Arsenal, in which was a very good performance by the team as a whole. The players showed a remarkable mental strength when not once, but twice, Arsenal equalised few moments after LFC scored 1-0, and

2-1. They kept pushing, kept trying, and ended up winning the game, with the attacking force of Adorjan, Suso, Ibe and Morgan being a real threat.

At the other end of the pitch, Ward did his work, showing how he is able to make remarkable saves, avoiding "inevitable" goals, and thus winning points and matches for the team. Even if he still makes the odd mistake and technical error, he has apparently lots of potential in him to become a real force in goal. In these early stages of his career it is obviously hard to predict any outcome, but he is definitely up there with the promising set of players up and coming from Melwood.

"Time will tell" is another aphorism, which means nothing or means everything at all. Time will tell if Rodgers is able to steer the team in the right direction, adding consistency to the performances; time will tell how many players of the current U21 squad will make it to the first team and help bringing silverware back to Anfield.

40.- Player selection and game plan

Date: 18/04/13
Previous matches: Reading 0-0 LFC (Premier League)

At this point in the season, there is little controversy regarding the best starting eleven for LFC; since the closing of last transfer window, the team sheet has been pretty stable, with no many voices raised about that selection.

Goalkeeper Reina and back four Johnson, Carragher, Agger and Enrique are nearly undoubtedly the best choice in the current squad. And they have been performing fairly well, especially in the defending side of their job. In midfield, both Leiva and Gerrard's places in the team look undisputable, Leiva as holding midfielder and Gerrard as a playmaker.

Attacking players Suarez, Sturridge and Coutinho are also almost automatic choices, even if Sturridge has been struggling as of late after a scintillating starting to his LFC career; but even so he has no real replacement in the squad in this moment, so either as a striker or as a wide player, the team needs to count on him. Coutinho and Suarez are the real threat posed on the pitch by LFC in last games, and both are decisive pillars of the team.

Hence, only one place in the team seems to be really into question in this stage of the season. The selection of that last player will ultimately determine the scheme of the team. Should that last player be Allen (now injured, so ineligible), it would imply a 4-3-3 with the three midfielders playing 2-1, so to speak, with Leiva as holding midfielder, Allen in an organising capacity, and Gerrard in a freer, more attacking, role; should that last player be Henderson, it would mean, in principle, those midfielders playing kind of 1-2, with Gerrard more devoted to midfield and Henderson being the more attacking midfielder; the choice of Downing would determine that the team was going to play in a more or less 4-2-3-1 scheme.

All of this, needless to say, generally speaking, and with subjection to the developments of the game. Game tactics are way more complicated and cannot be exhausted in just one paragraph, but those schemes are a useful way of speaking and dealing with these issues, in trying to understand how the team is trying to play, how the players will be deployed on the pitch.

There is nothing wrong in having different alternatives to approach the different games, the different opposition teams. In fact there is much good in having the alternatives, in being an adaptable team. The problem we are seeing in last matches is that Rodgers seems to need an extra player to play the way he wants to.

He seems to favour playing with three attacking midfielders, including two wingers and a player in the hole, supporting one forward. But, at the same time, he seems to want three players in midfield to ensure the control of the game, and of the possession of the football, the type of play he wants to display.

And Rodgers cannot have it both ways if he wants to keep the back four (and a goalkeeper). During February, March, and April, LFC have been playing probably its best and worst periods of football of the season. Sometimes the team has looked almost unstoppable. With the front four at full strength and being able to keep good control of the game, LFC have been a joy to watch at times; in other occasions, three midfielders have complemented well and been able to attack as well as dictate the rhythm of the game, and the team has been equally impressive.

Often during the same games, there have been other moments in which only two midfielders have been not enough to control the game, and the front four have been almost irrelevant; or in which three midfielders have not supported adequately the forwards with the result of losing the potential to inflict real damage to the opposition.

Probably balancing those aspects is the structural challenge LFC are facing now; and some progress has been shown, while some problems still remain. Last attempt, in the match against Reading, was playing Henderson as a left wing in a 4-2-3-1 scheme. In the best scenario, it would have resulted in Henderson adding to midfield when controlling the game while adding to the attack from the left flank; in the worst scenario, it would have resulted in effectively losing one player.

As seen on the pitch, that attempt was not fully successful. Similar to what happened in previous matches, LFC were brilliant at times and looked a little bit lost at other times, and Henderson was not particularly influent in the game, both in the good and in the bad spells.

However, in the long term, that does not appear to be a good solution. Playing Henderson out of position does not seem to be what the team needs. He is not a left wing, he is not even a left midfielder, and while a good player that can do a job wherever on the pitch, Henderson has had his best moments for the team in the centre, not on the wings.

It is difficult (in fact, impossible) to say what would have happened should Rodgers has played Downing, Suso, Sterling, Ibe,…instead of Henderson from the start of the match. But, judging from the last half an hour, in which Downing substituted Henderson, the team showed maybe some improvement towards the end of the game; but, as it was probably expected, there was certain decline in control of the game shortly after the substitution and certain gain in creating goal changes as the game was approaching its end.

That substitution, and indeed the very fact that it was the only substitution for LFC in the game, reinforced the ideas that, with Allen out for the season due to an injury, only twelve players are in contention. But it would probably be a good thing to make the choice coherently with the game plan. Either play three midfielders, and hence Henderson as a proper midfielder, or play with a front four, and hence Downing as wing.

Both have its pros and cons, and can obviously be combined during a game via the substitutions. But neither playing Henderson on the wing nor playing Downing as midfielder will, in the long term, do the trick.

Having said it all, it may be just fair to stress that LFC did more than enough to win the game against Reading, and only an almost superhuman performance by Reading goalkeeper prevented them to win, and even win comfortably. It was a much improved performance after the West Ham 0-0.

The remaining games of the season should serve as occasions to keep looking for that balance between keeping control of the game and attacking at full force. Those same games might also serve as occasions for bringing more players into the team, expanding the depth of the squad.

Either way, coherence between player selection and game plan will be a valuable asset in the long term.

41.- Taking the difficult path

Date: 26/04/13
Previous matches: LFC 2-2 Chelsea (Premier League); Chelsea U18 2-1 LFC U18 (FA Youth Cup)

Before the match, the game against Chelsea and the final games of the season looked difficult enough for LFC. Chelsea was a good team, with very good players and the additional emotional charge of Benitez at the bench; a good team fighting for that all important top four spot, as motivated as they come.

LFC faced a final run of the season with little chances of getting to fifth position, and the perspective of surpassing Everton in the table as the only specific motivation. The only, that is, in terms of "objective" meaningful achievements.

On the other hand, Chelsea provides always a big incentive for LFC, particularly over last years. And, more importantly, LFC should really aim at winning every game, no matter what. That is a sign of great teams, feeling obligation to win each time they play a game. Something that is time and again repeated in public statements by players and staff, but that is not always seen in performances on the pitch; something that is part and parcel of what LFC mean.

At least in the game against Chelsea, one cannot fault LFC players for lack of commitment. Each one fought like it was their last game, and LFC always looked the most motivated side; LFC players did everything in their power to win the game, especially in a scintillating second half.

Hence, no complaints on the attitude side. Even if players might have seemed a little bit flat in the first half, it was more than likely due to lack of inspiration, not lack of motivation. On the footballing side there were ups and downs, but overall the team looked the better side on the day. It was not a case of a total demolition of the opposition, but LFC were better.

However, a draw was all that was achieved. And thanks to a very, very late goal, in literally the last action of the game. A game ending up in a not totally fair result is not a rare thing in football. But the way in which the game unfolded conveyed the sense that LFC players did not think the task was difficult enough, and decided to make things more "interesting" by way of making things even harder for themselves.

Both in the match itself and in the league as a whole. Suarez biting to Ivanovic meant that season is over for the best LFC player of the season. The absurdity of the action makes it difficult even to ponder what would be the proper punishment. Ten matches look certainly harsh, but, obviously, the fact that Suarez was going to lose the remainder of the season was a foregone conclusion. With that biting LFC lost its best player for a string of games; and Suarez lost his chances both for being the league top scorer and, likely, for being voted as the best player of the season. All in a single, unexplainable, action. Suarez and the club will need to thoroughly work on the issue; Suarez is going to be challenged in every match by defenders trying to trigger similar response, so he will have to learn to deal with those situations. In the meantime, LFC will have to learn to deal without him with the following matches.

As for the Chelsea match, LFC also made things difficult for themselves. After and excellent start to the second half, with the victory for LFC the only likely outcome, Suarez punched the ball in Reina's box in what was less reprehensible, but almost as unexplainable, as his biting. In what was a poorly defended corner kick, worst case scenario was a Chelsea header from close distance that was potentially dangerous, but not nearly as dangerous as a penalty. Even so, Suarez left the referee with little option but pointing to the penalty spot.

That second Chelsea goal stopped a brilliant display of football by LFC, unplayable in those first ten minutes of the second half. It took a while for LFC players to come to terms with that goal. However, they eventually recovered, and more than deserved, at the very least, the draw.

But that second goal was not the only defensive mistake by LFC. The first goal, in which Oscar freely headed home from close range, was another very poorly defended corner kick. Something that has been a problem during all season for all LFC teams, from U18s to senior team and including U21s.

Word has it that the pre-season after Benitez left Valencia, the players asked his successor Ranieri in training how they should defend the corner kicks; Ranieri answered that, for the time being, they could go on the same way as the previous season. And the players answered that the previous season they had five different ways of defending corner kicks, depending on the opposition, the situation, the players on the field,...

In all likelihood there is no need for a team to have five different ways to defend corner kicks, but LFC teams will need to devote some time in following weeks and months to improve their defending in such situations that could be decisive at times. Not only the first team was prevented from winning by corner kicks; in the Youth FA Cup Chelsea also scored from a corner kick, drawing the match just before half time.

All truth be said, Chelsea were far superior in that match and worthy winners of the game and Youth FA Cup finalists. LFC players, hard as they tried, could not match the physical prowess of Chelsea players. It was probably good to have such a match to be aware of the room for improvement in a team used to better almost all of the opposition teams.

Also true is that both teams, senior and U18s, showed some very good things in their matches. In the occasions they were able to put the football on the ground and exchange passes and attack, LFC youngsters managed to seriously threat Chelsea defenders, and they might have scored more.

The first team was above Chelsea almost for the entire match, especially in a great second half. Their start to the second half, with Sturridge taking the game by storm, showed an unstoppable team, creating clear cut chances almost at will; after Chelsea second goal there was a period of recovering. But then, even if not at the high level of the previous moments, LFC completed a more than good second half, in which the second goal was coming time and again. That it would need to wait until the last touch of the game was more a case of bad luck than good luck for LFC.

LFC made its life difficult in the match with self infringed damage in the poor defending of corner kicks and for future games with Suarez biting. But the players also proved that they can compete and that they have chances to keep improving and build on the steps forward taken this season, even if they will need to stop making things more difficult than they already are, and to stop taking the difficult path to victory.

42.- The hero that was on time

Date: 16/05/13
Previous matches: Newcastle 0-6 LFC (Premier League); LFC 0-0 Everton (Premier League); Fulham 1-3 LFC (Premier League)

As scholars studying the mythology of Ancient Greece heroes have shown, one stand-out trait of those heroes is that they were seldom on time during their lives. The hero is usually not on time when he performs his extraordinary deeds in life. Only in a very special occasions were the Greek heroes on time, and that is something that presides over their entire life.

Last Sunday against Fulham LFC had its own hero, a hero that was precisely on time repeatedly during the match. It was one of such special occasions in which a hero is at the right place in the right moment. Sturridge recklessly hit Fulham until the victory was assured for LFC.

The start to the match was mainly uneventful, with LFC having the majority of ball possession and territory advantage, but without really threatening Schwarzer, whereas Fulham made some attempts but were not a real threat to Reina either. Getting close to halftime, Fulham was being increasingly daring, and they scored the opening in their first real chance.

That could have meant a harsh blow to LFC players, more so in an away match with no real significance in terms of the league table. It could have meant a blow, but it did not, thanks to the hero appearing just on time. Almost out of nowhere (a long ball, vaguely directed to him) Sturridge got the equaliser straight away, thus preventing the match to settle with Fulham advantage in the score.

In the second half Sturridge was again very much on time. Fulham were having a good period, and had a penalty claim in LFC box; shortly after that, Sturridge scored his second goal of the match, giving LFC a much appreciated lead. Those were the main timely appearances of that LFC hero of the match, even if his third goal helped to have a calm end to the match.

The fact of the decisiveness of the hero intervention in a football match does not diminish the importance of the analysis of other, more global, aspects of the match. In the end, a hero can only act when he has the backing of his fellow Greeks; or football team-mates, in this case.

The timely hero was only one of the contradictions in the match. Right from the start it could be seen that Rodgers had opted for playing three centre-backs; it was not his first time, but it was the first time in a while. Whether it had something to do with the illness of Skrtel is difficult, if not impossible, to know, but there they were, Wisdom, Carragher and Coates with Johnson and Downing with the whole wings at their disposal.

That formation inevitably weakens the defence of the crosses from the wings; that is something known and assumed as a price for having well covered the centre of the defence. However, not only Fulham players managed to put a good cross in LFC box, but Berbatov headed it home comfortably, with almost no opposition from LFC defenders. One lone striker on the box, three defenders there, and in went the ball.

It is the kind of mistake that could mark the difference in a match; this time, fortunately, it was not costly, but it needs to be avoided. Victories come with the chance to learn from irrelevant mistakes. But, it being the first goal of the match, it could have been relevant.

An easy header in front of three centre-backs was another contradiction of the match. The formation Rodgers chose for the first half made every sense in the idea of having the control of the match through the midfield, and ball possession. And indeed it worked at times during the first half. LFC had comfortably the majority of possession and played mostly on Fulham half.

However, LFC's only goal in that half came from a long ball. With long possessions all LFC players could really achieved was to control the rhythm and tempo of the game, but those possessions did not really lead to goal chances. In fact, it was Fulham the team that scored after a relatively long spell on the football.

Hence, the half time arrived with a draw achieved by the team with less time on the ball scoring after a long combination; the team with three centre-backs receiving a goal from a free header inside the box; the team that intended to control possession scoring through a long ball.

Further than that, LFC showed some encouraging signs in playing the game with ambition, in aiming at controlling the game; but also some not so encouraging signs, in lacking aggression in defence, in not putting enough pressure on Fulham players, in no recovering the football as soon and as high up on the pitch as could have been expected.

In the second half LFC played since the start with a more classical formation with two centre-backs and two full-backs, with Enrique taking to the pitch in the place of Wisdom and Downing switching to right midfield. In a sense, this second half was even more contradictory than the first. LFC opted for using much more often the counterattack, allowing Fulham to keep the ball while LFC were waiting for the chance to attack through quick transitions.

With this approach, LFC attacked, in a way, less; but at the same time created far more danger to Fulham goal. Apart from Sturridge's two goals in the half, there were at least 3 or 4 clear cut goal chances for LFC, way more than in the first half in which LFC largely dominated the game. That is of course good news, to be able to capitalise on counter attack chances; but, in order to keep progressing to become a real force LFC need to improve its attack against fully formed defences.

If that part of the game is not improved, it will be difficult to achieve the consistency needed to pose a credible challenge not only for the title, but even for a top four finishing. As showed in last games, playing like that will lead to big margin victories (6-0 against Newcastle, 3-1 against Fulham) but also frequent frustrating draws (0-0 against Everton, against Reading, against West Ham).

Improving the attack against formed defences, including turning long possessions into goal chances, while keeping the ability to hit in the counter attack when the occasion arises, would be the ideal scenario for next season.

That, and of course the emergence of the contradictory heroes that are on time, heroes that can turn the team efforts into goals, that can have impact on the score sheet when particularly needed, in the defining moments of the matches.

44.- Woodwork, again

Date: 21/05/13
Previous matches: LFC 1-0 QPR (Premier League)

Over last seasons LFC fans have been growing convinced that woodwork has been one of the principal factors standing in the way of the team, preventing it from getting much better results. I don't have with me statistics supporting or refuting that perception, but I also have the feeling that LFC are being more damaged by woodwork than other teams, and not only for a few matches, but over various seasons.

This recently ended 2012/13 season has been probably one in which woodwork has had less presence in LFC matches. However, it became an uninvited guess at the latch game, when Carragher managed to direct at goal a wonderful strike, beating the goalkeeper only to see it violently hitting the woodwork, thus preventing an even more glorious farewell for the Bootle defender.

At least Carragher walked out his last match having leading the defence to yet another clean sheet, rounding off what has been a remarkable end to the season for LFC as a team and for Carragher as a player. While he has not scored (not exactly a oddity in his career), on the league season as a whole LFC have received 30 goals in 22 matches without Carragher starting the games and 13 goals in 16 games with Carragher in the initial eleven. Moreover, many of those 13 goals came in his first matches back in the team; in his last seven games there have been 5 clean sheets and a total of 3 goals against.

This is one of those occasions in which statistics back what the eye of the fan perceives. LFC defence has been far more solid since Carragher returned to the team past January. Many things have been said, and rightly so, about the impact the two January signings, Coutinho and Sturridge, have had on the team. But, to tell the whole story, Carragher should be taken into the equation as a third January signing, in terms of his own impact on the team.

An impact that would have been great to see reflected in the score sheet in his last official match through that strike that woodwork stopped. But an impact that can be seen not only in terms of goals against, but also, more importantly, in terms of league points: from 30 points in 21 matches prior to mid January (taking out the 1-1 against Chelsea in November in which Carragher started) to 30 points in 15 matches since then (taking out the 3-1 March defeat against Southampton in which Carragher did not play).

Not that everything in that stark improvement can be attributed to Carragher. As said before, Coutinho and Sturridge have also played and important part in it. And other players, too, have improved their level during the second half of the season. The team as a whole has been gradually adapting to Rodgers' methods and ideas, and Rodgers himself has been settling into the club, the squad and even the city.

Even so, it is only fair to single out the performances of those "three January signings". Carragher has added to the defence, Coutinho has settled strikingly fast into the team, and improved the link between midfield and attack, and Sturridge has definitely provided goals to the team.

On the last game of the season Carragher and Coutinho delivered as usual, with solidity in the defence and the decisive goal in attack, in what was an only average performance of the team. Sturridge was far less involved in the game than in his better matches. And more or less as involved as in his worse matches.

One aspect of his game Sturridge needs to improve, and almost certainly will improve, is the consistency, the ability to perform near his best level in successive games. Having not played football with regularity until joining LFC, he is understandably finding it difficult to maintain his better performance level week in week out. Hopefully he is going to achieve that sooner than later.

Last game of the season, last game of Carragher, was also a first game. Jordon Ibe, 17, who was born only months before Carragher made his debut for LFC first team, made his own debut for the first team, and even opened his statistics with an assist for Coutinho's goal. He did OK during the match, though he was not as brilliant as he has been during the season for Academy teams.

Only time will tell where, and when, Ibe will get in his football career. As of now, he is living his dream, having appeared for the first team after starting the season with the U18s. He has had a tremendous season, and fully deserved his debut. He looks a great prospect for the future, though he needs to keep on working to reach his full potential. At least he has had his first taste of Premier League football, and seemed fairly settled and confident.

The last match of 12/13 season will surely be remembered for LFC as the last game of Carragher; and, if things go extremely well in the future, it could also be remembered as the first game of Ibe. But we are very far away from that as of now. Other than that, it was not a game to remember for any other thing. LFC dominated the game, were comfortable on the ball, and the result was never in doubt after the goal by Coutinho.

A great goal that in effect decided the match. LFC did not look particularly interested in scoring many more goals, and QPR did not look even capable of approaching LFC box with any danger. The kind of match that so often has ended with the opposition getting the equaliser and frustrating LFC while taking points from Anfield.

This time that did not happen. It would have been good if LFC closed the game with at least another goal. But that did not happen, either. And, while it is true that the team did not do a great deal to deserve that second goal, it is also true that woodwork can be deemed responsible not only for denying the team that second goal (which is not very important, given that the match ended with LFC winning) but also for denying Carragher his farewell goal, one that would have ended his illustrious Anfield career even more illustriously.

What woodwork could not do is diminish in the slightest the stature of Carragher not only as a legend; but as a legend retiring near his peak, while having been the best defender of the season for the team.

CONCLUSION.- Player by player season assessment

Trying to take an overall look on the season, it may make sense to have a brief view over how each player has performed. With the inevitable limits of keeping if brief and simple, here is a tentative assessment:

Reina: coming from a couple of seasons below his best level, he started the season with well below par performances, and he even lost, for the first time in LFC, several games due to injuries. In the second half of the season, with more regularity, he improved his game, and got close to what he showed in his first seasons.

Jones: he has been called into action more often than any substitute goalkeeper in several LFC seasons, especially during the first half of the season. He did well, kept his performances at a good level, and was as good a replacement goalkeeper as one could ask for. However, he does not seem to be good enough to be the first choice goalie for LFC.

Johnson: he has had one good season in terms of the amount of games played, having avoided most of his recurrent physical troubles. He has been a reliable player, consistently performing well. Even so, his outstanding attacking ability has been seen in little doses. Keeping the consistency while adding more brilliant appearances in attack would make him an even greater asset to the team. Good season for him, overall.

Enrique: lots of ups and downs for him. In a bad starting to the season, an injury prevented him from really performing at his best. After completing his recovery, he had some very good games in midfield before coming back to full back. He struggled to find the right balance between the defensive and the attacking sides of his game, but he has been a good, even if not brilliant, player.

Agger: consistent player, solid performances. He has been injury-free for most of the season, which has added very much to the defensive reliability of the team. His technical quality makes him a valuable help to midfielders in building the ball-possession game. He probably could be more involved in the game, but he has had a good season.

Carragher: irrespective of his standing as a club legend for his many years of service, he has had a terrific season. He has been the best defender of the squad, and a great figure in the massive defensive improvement in the defensive side of the team during the second half of the season. He has retired being a key member of the squad even if only for his performances in the 12/13 season.

Wisdom: he had many games at the beginning of the season, and was a solid defender as right back. Still, doubts remain regarding his potential as right back. He has been a central defender in the Academy for years, and might be a better asset there. However, during 12/13 he has been a solid, consistent, right back, but several steps below Johnson and the level required for a top team player.

Skrtel: an ever-present defender in the first half of the season, he lost his place in the team to Carragher from January, and rightly so, since Carragher proved to be a much better player. Skrtel can be, at most, a good replacement, a good squad member, but not a regular in the team.

Coates: he has had very limited opportunities in the first team. Not enough to really make a judgement; even so, at his age a decision should be made by the staff regarding his long term status in the squad, and whether or not he has what it takes to make it to the top level.

Kelly: good start to the season, but a very early, long term, injury kept him in the sidelines.

Leiva: a solid season for him. After his second consecutive long term injury, he has been improving during the season, and has completed a good second half of the season. Still a little bit short of being a real top class player as a holding midfielder, he is a reliable player.

Allen: after a brilliant start to the season, he has failed to really develop the full potential that sometimes he seems to have in him. He looked kind of shy, restricting himself to the distribution of the ball from defence. He needs to widen his influence in the game, to step up and really command matches, if he is to make a real impact in top level.

Gerrard: great season for LFC captain. Almost ever present, sometimes deeper, sometimes higher up the pitch, he has stamped his authority in many matches. Not as brilliant as some years ago, but almost equally as important in his new role. He has proved his football wisdom and continued to help the team almost everywhere on the pitch.

Henderson: much improved in his second season in the team. Even more, he has kept improving during the season, becoming more adapted to the team. He has added some goals to his contribution. Doubts remain, however, about whether or not he is really a player the size required by LFC. More useful in the centre of the pitch than on the wings.

Shelvey: a contradictory season for him. He has showed some glimpses of a real great player, and some impressive performances, while also lacking consistency and reliability. He struggles with turning his potential into real achievements. He is still young, but up to now is only a squad player who has not fully proved a proper regularity in his game. Hopefully he will be able to keep growing as a player.

Downing: similar to Henderson, his second season has been much better than his first one. He has been a good player, providing needed width to the team, and has improved his understanding with the rest of the players, helping with defence and construction of the game. Still, he does not seem to be a top class winger.

Suso: a good start to the season, showing good actions and being a type of player much needed by the team, with an eye for defence-splitting passes. He almost disappeared from the team in second half of the season. A promising player, good resource to count on, not fully ready as of now.

Sterling: a radiant appearance at the beginning of the season. He seemingly settled in the first team with ease. Little by little, the amount of minutes on the pitch took their toll, and he needed rest, being almost unused in the second half of the season. Being quick and able to create problems to defenders, he has time on his side to keep improving, adding knowledge of the game, good quality crosses, and scoring ability. Time will tell if he is able to fulfil his potential. Still a player in the making.

Coutinho: the real star of the team since his arrival in January. A top class player, excellent technique, capable of scoring goals, of offering passes and goals to other players, of associating in midfield, of dribbling defenders,...He has been a real success since the very beginning. He sometimes looks lost during the matches, so he will need to improve the continuity of his game, and his confidence in imposing his ability. There are some spells in which he seems absent from the game, so he needs to be more of a constant presence in the matches. A great signing, if he can confirm in the future what he has shown in his first months.

Sturridge: another great addition in January. A much needed striker that can be an accurate finisher and also help with creating passes and building the game, linking with midfielders. He shone at certain games while in other games were almost invisible, and even needed to rest at times. He will need to get used to playing games in quick succession. But he seems to be a good piece in Rodgers' scheme.

Suarez: yet again, another excellent season, marred by unsporting behaviour. As a player, at least in the top three of the Premier League, and maybe even the best. He works tirelessly for the team, beats defenders, creates goals for himself, finishes goals created by others. He can play as a lone striker or in the hole behind a forward, or from the wings. He could play everywhere and do everything if only he could apply restraint to his non-footballing actions. But, as a player, outstanding season.

Borini: a promising signing, he spent most of the season injured. If and when fully fit, he might add needed depth to the squad, with his goal scoring capabilities. As for 12/13 season, injuries prevented him from really showing what he is capable of.

The team as a whole has had a contradictory season, intended from the beginning to be just a first step in a long term building process. In that sense, it is true that some significant progress has been made, and has been seen on the pitch. At the beginning of the season, Rodgers tried to change the way of playing somewhat abruptly, with mixed results. Little by little, he was adjusting his ideas to the players, resulting in a more successful second half of the season, with less short passes and more long passes.

Whether or not clubs the size of LFC can, or may, accept these transitional, almost ambitionless, seasons is a matter of opinion. More important is the question of the potential for the team to keep progressing, and if the path chosen is the right one. At the very least, Rodgers has been able to convey a sense of purpose in his actions, a long term plan to take LFC where it belongs. A sense of direction that had been missed in last years, and that is key to a future success. Future achievements will reveal the extent to which 12/13 season has been more of a failure or more of a success.

Printed in Great Britain
by Amazon.co.uk, Ltd.,
Marston Gate.